MW00460612

# The PASTOR'S HANDBOOK
## Revised Edition
### King James Version

---

*Instructions, forms and helps
for conducting the many ceremonies
a minister is called upon to direct*

---

*WingSpread Publishers*
*Chicago, Illinois*

*WingSpread Publishers*
*Chicago, Illinois*

www.moodypublishers.com

*An imprint of Moody Publishers*

*The Pastor's Handbook*
Revised KJV Edition
ISBN: 978-1-60066-139-6
LOC Catalog Card Number: 2006901538
© 1958, 1963, 1986, 1988, 2003 by Christian Publications, Inc.


Previously published by Christian Publications, Inc.
First Christian Publications edition 1958
Revised KJV edition 2003
First WingSpread Publishers edition 2006

9  10  8

Scripture taken from the
Holy Bible: King James Version.

Purchasers of this manual may copy any of the
liturgies for the purpose of appropriate audience
participation in the several ceremonies

# Contents

# Preface

> *To know what to say and how to say it—what finer gift could a clergyman possess?*
>
> —Charles Perkins

*T*HE PASTOR'S HANDBOOK IS INTENDED to meet the continuing need of the Christian minister for guidance and forms as he does the work of the ministry. It seeks to offer options to suit the tastes of pastor and congregation within the parameters of quality, beauty and dignity. To this end, numerous changes, both large and small, have been made—more selected Scriptures, new alternatives for special occasions, some significant additions and changes. At the same time, every effort has been made to keep the book concise and compact to maximize its usefulness.

The formulas should be sufficient for the ordinary needs of the minister. They may be modified or supplemented by materials from the pastor's private collection or of his own preparation.

Some who stress liberty in prayer and preaching dislike set forms, preferring spontaneity and a free style as they worship. If the spiritual vitality of a church is maintained, there need be no fear that these forms will become lifeless ritual. The use of forms should never become merely formal. And if the use of such forms adds beauty and dignity to the atmosphere of sacredness, who can object?

WingSpread Publishers gratefully acknowledges the invaluable input of the following people into this revision of *The Pastor's Handbook*: Joseph Arthur, Robert C. Bashioum, Elio Cuccaro, Charles W. Davis, Jr., Arnold R. Fleagle, K. Neill Foster, W.R. Goetz, Paul B. Hazlett, David R. King, Kenneth M. Toczyski and Leon W. Young.

Gratitude is also expressed to those who contributed to earlier editions: Richard W. Bailey, Paul F. Bubna, Carl S. McGarvey, C.E. Mock, John E. Stevey, W. David Thomas, Robert C. Bashioum, Arnold R. Fleagle, Edwin H. Henning, Mark L. Howard, David Hustad, J. Arnold Johnson, Jeffrey A. Mackey, Nathan B. Penland Jr. and Martin I. Webber. To each one, the publisher is indebted.

May the blessing of God attend all who glean from this manual, enabling them to know what to say and how to say it, what to do and how to do it, as occasion may require.

# 1 • The Pastor

WHO, MORE THAN THE MINISTER, touches people in their most solemn and sacred moments? Whether he is asked to dedicate a baby, unite young adults in marriage, counsel a hurting father or bury an aged saint, the pastor has the holy privilege of ministering the grace of Christ Jesus to those he lives among. Therefore:

The pastor must see to his spirit. He must keep the fires of devotion to his God burning brightly. The Word must be his delight and prayer his chief business. Only as he keeps in contact with the Throne can he be God's emissary.

He must avoid empty professionalism—the bane of every minister—at all cost. His ministry is important to those who look to him for help; it must be important to him, too.

In his concern for the household of God, the pastor must not neglect his own household. If he has a wife, the marriage vows he mediates to others are the vows he himself took. If he has children, they are as sacred a trust as any other in his parish—and more so because the responsibility is uniquely his.

The pastor should be careful about his personal appearance. Cleanliness may not be next to godliness, but it ranks nearby. Whatever the limitations of his wardrobe, his clothes should enhance the dignity of his calling. Nothing on or about him should clamor for attention.

1

The minister must also have the proper manner. Gravity need not be gloom, and seriousness is not necessarily sadness. The pastor's manner will reflect the importance of the occasion. The King's business calls for a kingly bearing. Quiet reserve is always the mark of a Christian man. The pastor should act in such a way that no one will ever regret having sought his assistance. Manner is the sum total of manners.

Those who are called by Jesus Christ to His ministry are called to be good ministers. No man could be more. Who dares to be less?

# 2 • *The Worship Service*

THE WORSHIP SERVICE CREATES an atmosphere where individual believers interact with a transcendent God within a covenant community. Worship forms may vary with cultures or generations, but the content remains unchanged. At least four principles regulate the content of the worship service.

1. *Worship is not something we attend; it is something we do. It is a corporate gathering to exalt our worthy God for His mighty acts of salvation.* True worship, therefore, is participative. We gather not primarily to receive but to give. Worship is a heart attitude to be expressed in word and act. It is larger than any of the individual elements of the worship service. It is all the facets of the service in relation to the hearts of the worshipers.

2. *What we do in worship must be grounded in the Scriptures.* The Bible is our only rule of faith and practice. Both Old and New Testaments serve as authority and source for our times of worship. From these sacred sources we glean psalms, hymns, doxologies, benedictions, confessions, prayers, ascriptions of glory and patterns of worship.

3. *What we do in worship must always be oriented toward Christ—particularly in His redemptive work.* The early Church centered its preaching and worship in what we call the *kerygma*—the proclamation of Christ—His birth, life, sufferings, death, resurrection, ascension. Worship praises God the Father for this redemption in Jesus Christ His Son and reenacts it in the ordinances of the Lord's Supper and Baptism.

4. *The forms of our worship are rooted in both the Jewish temple/synagogue and in the early Church.* Our worship comprises both the commonality of those forms and their distinctives. Our worship is rooted in the liturgy and pageantry of temple worship, but also in the spontaneity of the early Church. Worship is both sacramental and free.

## AN ORDER FOR "FREE" WORSHIP

**Preparation:** As worshipers arrive, they may be given intercessory suggestions for quiet prayer. Worship choruses may be sung spontaneously or under a leader's direction. If spontaneously, bear in mind that visitors unfamiliar with the songs may feel estranged. Printed Scriptures help each worshiper focus on a particular theme for the worship time.

Worshipers may be called to self-examination and personal confession through the use of a hymn (sung or unsung), the naming of one of God's attributes or a specific Scripture.

**Hymns of praise:** Psalms set to music or Scripture songs may be committed to memory and sung. Hymns may be announced or spontaneously begun by the leader or worshipers. Both the Scripture songs and the hymns should point worshipers to God and His activity and attributes.

**Scripture:** Scriptures may be assigned to members of the congregation to read—or they may be read spontaneously. If assigned, use the whole Bible—Psalms and other Old Testament portions and passages from the Gospels, the Acts and the Letters. Members may be asked to quote memorized Scriptures that call attention to some aspect of the person and work of Christ Jesus.

The worship leader may wish to acknowledge that these Scriptures are the inspired Word of God, demanding our undivided attention. They have the power of

God through the Holy Spirit to convey truth, correction and the assurance of eternal life.

**Intercessory prayer:** The pastor may lead the congregation in prayer for needs within the local fellowship of believers and ministries around the world. He may on occasion call on any who so desire to offer spontaneous prayers. Or he may lead a time of directed prayer, asking people to pray silently or audibly for specific needs, which he announces one by one. But remember, for the initiated, directed prayer can be an effective change of pace; for strangers, it can be awkward and meaningless.

**Offering:** The offering, frequently regarded by pastor and congregation as an interruption, should be seen rather as an important part of congregational worship. Even as the members present themselves to God in His sanctuary, so they present their offerings—the fruit of their daily labor—as a love gift to God and His kingdom work. An offering receptacle positioned so worshipers may place their gifts as they enter the sanctuary is customary in some churches. But certainly the corporate reception of tithes and offerings at a given point in the worship service can and should be a fitting act of worship. On occasion, the offering may be placed after the sermon as a congregational response to God's Word.

**Sermon:** Several elements may be incorporated into the preparation for the Word or the declaration of the Word, including drama, storytelling or media aids such as slides, videos or graphics. The communications revolution which has moved from the ancient method of oral presentation to the contemporary availability of audiovisual aids permits a broad assortment of tools to be employed in the presentation of God's Word. There can be no substitute, however, for anointed preaching with power.

**Response:** Every sermon should call for some listener response. The audience may be given opportunity to respond in a variety of ways, but each worshiper should be specifically challenged to respond.

An evangelistic sermon should be followed by an invitation to repent and confess Christ publicly as Savior and Lord. The appropriate response may be to personal commitment, with an invitation to the worshipers to demonstrate right then their assent. Depending on the sermon theme, the response may be to write a note of encouragement to someone, to attend or join a prayer group, to make a faith promise to missions or to read privately some portion of Scripture.

**The Lord's Table:** If communion is to be observed, it is appropriate to schedule it as a part of the response. (See chapter 3, "Communion.")

**Close:** A hymn or Scripture song in keeping with the theme of the service, followed possibly by a benediction, will fitly conclude the worship time.

## AN ORDER FOR
## MORE FORMAL WORSHIP

**Preparation:** Scriptures may be included in the printed Order of Worship for meditation before the service formally begins. An appropriate prelude of hymns and gospel songs will help to set the tone of the service. A painting, banners, projected pictures or other non-verbal forms of communication may be used to focus the attention of the worshipers.

**Announcements:** These should not be considered unimportant. Rather the participatory events which the announcements describe are often the sinews that bind the body together.

**Call to worship:** The choir may call the congregation to worship through music, or the pastor or worship leader may do so with an appropriate Scripture or by leading the congregation in a unison or responsive reading of a printed declaration.

**Hymn of praise:** The opening hymn should speak to the nature or attributes of God and should be addressed to Him.

**Ascriptions of praise:** These may be personal, planned witness statements, or the pastor may use Scripture selections in keeping with the theme of the day. The congregation may sing the *Gloria*.

**Prayer of invocation:** This may be a Scripture invocation (see following pages) or a brief prayer in the pastor's own words invoking the manifest presence of God in the worship experience. On occasion, individuals within the congregation may be asked in advance to voice brief invocations.

**Old Testament Scripture:** The pastor or lay leader will choose a passage supportive of the theme of the worship service.

**Music:** A choral anthem or other special music may be included at this point.

**Offering:** Worshipers are given opportunity to present their tithes and offerings to God. An instrumental or vocal ministry may accompany the reception of the offering.

**Doxology and prayer of dedication**

**New Testament Scripture:** The pastor or lay leader will read a New Testament passage supportive of the day's worship theme.

**Pastoral prayer:** The pastoral prayer is opportunity for the minister, in his role of priest, to bear before God the praise of his people as well as to intercede for those members with particular needs. Conscientiously carried out, it can be a highlight of the service and a lasting benediction for the worshipers.

**Special music:** A song well executed and appropriate to the theme of the service can prepare the congregation for what follows and permit the pastor a brief time of quiet before he stands to minister the Word to his people.

**Sermon**

**Response:** The response may be a corporate recitation of the Apostles' Creed, a litany prepared and printed in the bulletin or an invitation to a public confession of faith or of dedication. A public witness, asked for well in advance, supportive of the sermon theme, may be offered by a member of the congregation. Some churches might even use drama to act out the response in life situations.

**Hymn of affirmation**

**Prayer of thanksgiving**

**Charge:** The pastor, in his charge to the congregation, may repeat the major theme of the worship time.

**Benediction:** See the end of this chapter for a collection of benedictions.

**Postlude:** The congregation may sing a chorus, or the organist may play a selection.

## HELPS FOR WORSHIP

**Use of color in worship services:** Throughout history, worship has been associated with symbols—crosses, altar Bibles, center pulpits, communion tables. Likewise, colors traditionally have been used to set the mood of the worship service. Colors that take on significance in the Christian calendar include:

**Violet,** the color used by kings in mourning. It symbolizes the majesty of Christ in His humility. It is used by the Church for the penitential seasons and, traditionally, was also used during Advent.

**Blue,** which is gradually replacing violet for Advent. Blue is the color of royalty, and therefore fittingly symbolizes the coming of Him who was born King.

**White,** the color of light. It symbolizes divinity, purity, victory. It is used for Christmas, Epiphany, Easter and Trinity Sunday.

**Green,** the common color of nature in the freshness of bloom. Symbolic of Christian life and growth, it is used during the many Sundays of the Trinity season.

**Red,** associated with blood and spirit. It is used on Pentecost and Reformation Sundays and in festivals such as Thanksgiving, anniversaries and dedications. It symbolizes the zeal of the Church, and it is used to commemorate the martyrs who sealed their testimony with their blood.

**Black,** the color of darkness and death. It is used on Good Friday.

### *Calls to worship*

Be still, and know that I am God: I will be exalted among the heathen, I will be exalted in the earth.

(Psalm 46:10)

Exalt the LORD our God, and worship at his holy hill; for the LORD our God is holy.

(Psalm 99:9)

O give thanks unto the LORD, for he is good: for his mercy endureth for ever. Let the redeemed of the LORD say so, whom he hath redeemed from the hand of the enemy.

(Psalm 107:1-2)

O praise the LORD, all ye nations: praise him, all ye people. For his merciful

kindness is great toward us: and the
truth of the LORD endureth for ever.
Praise ye the LORD.

(Psalm 117)

This is the day which the LORD hath
made; we will rejoice and be glad in it.

(Psalm 118:24)

I was glad when they said unto me,
Let us go into the house of the LORD.

(Psalm 122:1)

Praise ye the LORD. Praise God in his
sanctuary: praise him in the firmament
of his power. . . . Let every thing that
hath breath praise the LORD. Praise ye
the LORD.

(Psalm 150:1, 6)

But the LORD is in his holy temple:
let all the earth keep silence before him.

(Habakkuk 2:20)

Come unto me, all ye that labour and
are heavy laden, and I will give you rest.

(Matthew 11:28)

God is a Spirit: and they that worship him must worship him in spirit and in truth.

(John 4:24)

If ye then be risen with Christ, seek those things which are above, where Christ sitteth on the right hand of God. Set your affection on things above, not on things on the earth.

(Colossians 3:1-2)

*Invocations: These prayers may be easily expanded to include the entire congregation by changing the singular "I," "me" and "my" to "we," "us" and "our" and modifying the other parts of speech to show agreement.*

But as for me, I will come into thy house in the multitude of thy mercy: and in thy fear will I worship toward thy holy temple. Lead me, O LORD, in thy righteousness because of mine enemies; make thy way straight before my face.

(Psalm 5:7-8)

Unto thee, O LORD, do I lift up my soul. O my God, I trust in thee: let me not be ashamed, let not mine enemies triumph over me. Yea, let none that wait on thee be ashamed: let them be ashamed which transgress without cause.

(Psalm 25:1-3)

Shew me thy ways, O LORD; teach me thy paths. Lead me in thy truth, and teach me: for thou art the God of my salvation; on thee do I wait all the day. Remember, O LORD, thy tender mercies and thy lovingkindnesses; for they have been ever of old.

(Psalm 25:4-6)

LORD, I have loved the habitation of thy house, and the place where thine honour dwelleth. . . . My foot standeth in an even place: in the congregations will I bless the LORD.

(Psalm 26:8, 12)

I will praise thee, O Lord, among the people: I will sing unto thee among the nations. For thy mercy is great unto the heavens, and thy truth unto the clouds. Be thou exalted, O God, above the heavens: let thy glory be above all the earth.

(Psalm 57:9-11)

O God, thou art my God; early will I seek thee: my soul thirsteth for thee, my flesh longeth for thee in a dry and thirsty land, where no water is; to see thy power and thy glory, so as I have seen thee in the sanctuary. Because thy lovingkindness is better than life, my lips shall praise thee. Thus will I bless thee while I live: I will lift up my hands in thy name.

(Psalm 63:1-4)

How amiable are thy tabernacles, O LORD of hosts! My soul longeth, yea, even fainteth for the courts of the LORD: my heart and my flesh crieth out for the living God. . . . Blessed are they that dwell in thy house: they will be still praising thee.

(Psalm 84:1-2, 4)

Give ear, O LORD, unto my prayer; and attend to the voice of my supplications. In the day of my trouble I will call upon thee: for thou wilt answer me. Among the gods there is none like unto thee, O Lord; neither are there any works like unto thy works. All nations whom thou hast made shall come and worship before thee, O Lord; and shall glorify thy name. For thou art great, and doest wondrous things: thou art God alone.

(Psalm 86:6-10)

Unto thee lift I up mine eyes, O thou that dwellest in the heavens. Behold, as the eyes of servants look unto the hand of their masters, and as the eyes of a maiden unto the hand of her mistress; so our eyes wait upon the LORD our God, until that he have mercy upon us.

(Psalm 123:1-2)

### Offertory sentences

Offer unto God thanksgiving; and pay thy vows unto the most High: And call upon me in the day of trouble: I will deliver thee, and thou shalt glorify me.

(Psalm 50:14-15)

Give unto the LORD, O ye kindreds of the people, give unto the LORD glory and strength. Give unto the LORD the glory due unto his name: bring an offering, and come into his courts.

(Psalm 96:7-8)

Honour the LORD with thy substance, and with the firstfruits of all thine increase: So shall thy barns be filled with plenty, and thy presses shall burst out with new wine.

(Proverbs 3:9-10)

Bring ye all the tithes into the storehouse, that there may be meat in mine house, and prove me now herewith, saith the LORD of hosts, if I will not open you the windows of heaven, and pour you out a blessing, that there shall not be room enough to receive it.

(Malachi 3:10)

Upon the first day of the week let every one of you lay by him in store, as God hath prospered him.

(1 Corinthians 16:2)

## Benedictions

The LORD bless thee, and keep thee: The LORD make his face shine upon thee, and be gracious unto thee: The LORD lift up his countenance upon thee, and give thee peace.

(Numbers 6:24-26)

Now to him that is of power to stablish you according to my gospel, and the preaching of Jesus Christ, according to the revelation of the mystery, which was kept secret since the world began, but now is made manifest, and by the scriptures of the prophets, according to the commandment of the everlasting God, made known to all nations for the obedience of faith: To God only wise, be glory through Jesus Christ for ever. Amen.

(Romans 16:25-27)

The grace of the Lord Jesus Christ, and the love of God, and the communion of the Holy Ghost, be with you all. Amen.

(2 Corinthians 13:14)

Grace be to you and peace from God the Father, and from our Lord Jesus Christ, who gave himself for our sins, that he might deliver us from this present evil world, according to the will of God and our Father: To whom be glory for ever and ever. Amen.

(Galatians 1:3-5)

Now unto him that is able to do exceeding abundantly above all that we ask or think, according to the power that worketh in us, unto him be glory in the church by Christ Jesus throughout all ages, world without end. Amen.

(Ephesians 3:20-21)

And the very God of peace sanctify you wholly; and I pray God your whole spirit and soul and body be preserved blameless unto the coming of our Lord Jesus Christ.

(1 Thessalonians 5:23)

Now unto the King eternal, immortal, invisible, the only wise God, be honour and glory for ever and ever. Amen.

(1 Timothy 1:17)

Now the God of peace, that brought again from the dead our Lord Jesus, that great shepherd of the sheep, through the blood of the everlasting covenant, make you perfect in every good work to do his will, working in you that which is wellpleasing in his sight, through Jesus Christ; to whom be glory for ever and ever. Amen.

(Hebrews 13:20-21)

But the God of all grace, who hath called us unto his eternal glory by Christ Jesus, after that ye have suffered a while, make you perfect, stablish, strengthen, settle you. To him be glory and dominion for ever and ever. Amen.

(1 Peter 5:10-11)

Now unto him that is able to keep you from falling, and to present you faultless before the presence of his glory with exceeding joy, to the only wise God our Saviour, be glory and majesty, dominion and power, both now and ever. Amen.

(Jude 24-25)

Unto him that loved us, and washed us from our sins in his own blood, and hath made us kings and priests unto God and his Father; to him be glory and dominion for ever and ever. Amen.

(Revelation 1:5-6)

## *OCCASIONAL SUNDAYS*

Throughout the church year, there are not only the universally recognized religious holidays such as Easter and Christmas, but other significant days—Mother's Day, Pentecost and Thanksgiving, to name a few, as well as national holidays and even local commemorations of significance to the Church.

If the minister suits a sermon to all of these other occasional days, he will have few remaining Sundays to proclaim the whole counsel of God to his people. He should therefore take care that these occasional Sundays do not intrude on his systematic exposition of God's Word. If he preaches a message to mothers one year, he may wish to preach to fathers the next year—and to children the next. If his sermon one year is in keeping with Independence Day, he may decide to forgo a similar theme the next. It is possible to recognize special occasions in the course of a church service without devoting sermons to them.

The minister has a God-given responsibility to declare "all the counsel of God" (Acts 20:27), and he will look critically at any occasion or program that deprives his congregation of such comprehensive preaching.

# 3 • *Communion*

IN THE ORDINANCE OF COMMUNION, believers experience the most blessed and sacred bond between themselves and their risen Lord, and between one another. It merges heart and mind in devotion to the person and work of the Lord Jesus Christ. No other service so reflects the vital elements of Christian experience and faith. Let the pastor purpose to so understand its truth and direct its observance as to bring its holy significance within the experience of each participant every time it is observed.

The pastor will see that the preparation of the table and the elements is in the hands of responsible persons. Clean linens and clean communionware are indispensable. Those who assist should be properly attired and well informed as to what is expected of them and how the service is to proceed.

The place given to communion in a regular worship service is important. Let it never be an appendage to a service; let it never be unrelated to the theme of the service; let it never be observed with haste. Its holy character and spiritual content demand for communion the climactic point in the worship service. When it is to be observed, let all parts of the service contribute to its meaning. To this end, it is in order to have a communion meditation, a mini-sermon, before the elements are served.

The minister, in a gracious manner, will make it clear that the Lord's table is for the Lord's people—those born again and living a holy life. The Scriptures are clear that each person bears responsibility before God to determine his or her fitness to partake: "But let a man examine himself, and so let him eat of that bread, and drink of that cup" (1 Corinthians 11:28). But participation is not optional for the believer: "This do" (11:24).

While various religious bodies differ on who is allowed to participate in the Lord's Supper, The Christian and Missionary Alliance practices open communion. This means that adults make their own decisions about taking part, after being encouraged to appropriately examine themselves. In the case of families, parents should be allowed to determine when and if their children should receive the elements. If they know that their child has prayed to receive Christ and that he has a basic understanding of the symbolism involved, they should be free to allow their child to participate.

## SIMULTANEOUS COMMUNION

Because it heightens the sense of congregational unity, simultaneous communion is most commonly practiced. In this form, communicants retain the bread when they are served, and all partake together at a given signal. Likewise, the cup.

The minister will give the invitation to partake at the Lord's table, emphasizing its significance and seriousness. Those designated to serve—usually the elders—make an orderly and dignified approach to the table. Two or more of them may have been pre-instructed to remove and fold any covering linens.

From memory the minister quotes: "For I have received of the Lord that which also I delivered unto you, that the Lord Jesus the same night in which he was betrayed took bread: And when he had given thanks, he brake it, and said, Take, eat: this is my body, which is broken for you: this do in remembrance of me." (1 Corinthians 11:23-24).

At this point, the minister or one of the servers offers a prayer of thanks for the bread. Requesting the congregation to retain the bread so that all may partake together, the minister hands the plates containing the bread to the servers, who in turn move out in a predetermined pattern to distribute it. During the distribution of both bread and cup, the instrumentalist may play soft music, or the congregation may sing, or all may meditate quietly.

Upon the return of the servers to the table, the minister takes the bread plate from each and, still holding the last plate, serves the now seated servers. Taking a portion of bread for himself, the minister may quote Scripture or speak a sentence extemporaneously. Or he may prefer to offer the prayer of thanks for the bread at this point in the service. His words should be calculated to fix the hearts of the congregation on the Lord Jesus Christ in devotion, worship and adoration.

The pastor then invites participants to eat simultaneously. He will follow this with a brief silence for meditation.

Again quoting, the minister says: "After the same manner also he took the cup, when he had supped, saying, This cup is the new testament in my blood: this do ye, as oft as ye drink it, in remembrance of me. For as often as ye eat this bread, and drink this cup, ye do shew the Lord's death till he come" (11:25-26). Again he requests the congregation to wait for all to be served. The routine followed in the distribution of the bread is repeated with the trays of cups.

After all have been served, including those serving, the minister holds his cup and, after an appropriate

Scripture, remark or prayer, invites all to drink together. After a brief silence for meditation, the minister may conclude the communion time with prayer.

If holders are not provided in the pews for the empty glasses, the servers will return with the empty trays to collect them—or, if they are diposable glasses, ushers may be prepared with containers to pass through each pew.

It is appropriate and meaningful to incorporate a time of anointing with oil immediately following the communion service. Some churches have the elders stand up front and administer the anointing. Other churches invite individuals to stand in the aisles and the elders move to those locations.

Many churches have the custom of receiving a benevolent offering at the conclusion of the communion service. If that is the case, ushers should be prepared to receive this offering.

## COMMUNION AT THE ALTAR

Many churches customarily serve the emblems while participants kneel at the altar. Ushers may be enlisted to regulate the orderly flow of people to and from the altar, starting from the front, according to a prearranged pattern. Aged or infirm who find it difficult to kneel may be seated on a front pew to be served. Participants are first served the bread, then the cup, the minister commenting appropriately as he distributes the elements. He then concludes with a brief prayer before dismissing those kneeling in preparation for the next group.

## OTHER VARIATIONS

As a variation, all Scripture, commentary and prayer may precede the distribution of the elements. The elements may then be distributed in total silence, or with singing, testimony or recitation of Scripture, prose or poetry.

In place of the more customary broken bread, whole rolls or matzohs may be substituted, one for each row of worshiper. The servers hand the element to the **second** person in the pew, who offers the bread to the **first** person. After the first person has broken off a portion, the **second** person hands the loaf to the **third** person, who in turn serves the **second** person. A server at the far end of the pew will serve the last person and return any remaining part of the loaf to the table. Obviously, this observance requires clear instructions if it is to operate smoothly. Because of its involved nature, it might be better implemented in a smaller, more intimate setting than in a normal congregation.

Another variation is to let the entire worship service be conducted from the communion table. There is no formal sermon, but the minister discourses informally. Prayer, music and testimonies of praise fill out unhurried fellowship around the Lord's table. Minute preparation is absolutely necessary lest the service lack its essential elements.

Communion songs could be chosen which lead the congregation through the themes of death, resurrection and celebration, which encompass a journey through the meaning of the ordinance.

# 4 • Baptism

**B**APTISM, TOGETHER WITH COMMUNION, is one of the two ordinances enjoined by the Lord Jesus Christ upon believers. Unfortunately, Christians sometimes regard it as unimportant or even optional. The minister must therefore set forth the scriptural purpose of baptism in such a way that believers will see it not only as their privilege but their duty.

Christendom historically has practiced three modes of baptism: immersion, pouring and sprinkling. Some churches baptize the infant children of believing members. Immersion best depicts the concept of "buried with him by baptism into death: that like as Christ was raised up from the dead by the glory of the Father, even so we also should walk in newness of life" (Romans 6:4). Baptism is a believer's witness to others of the inner transformation effected by Jesus Christ. These instructions are therefore predicated upon that understanding.

The pastor and/or the church elders will take time with each candidate to assure themselves that the person is genuinely saved. They will ascertain that the candidate understands the meaning and purpose of the ordinance, and the pastor will inform the candidate just how the ceremony will proceed—the candidate, properly robed or clothed, will enter the water, face the congregation and, at the pastor's invitation, share his or her assurance of salvation through Jesus Christ. The candidate will then turn to the right and, as the minister begins the words "I baptize you . . ." he or she will clasp the minister's wrist

27

with both hands. The minister, holding a folded handkerchief over the candidate's nose and mouth and placing his other hand on the back of the candidate's shoulders, will lower him or her backward into the water. The minister will then assist the candidate to an upright position.

Prior to the service, assigned persons will make sure the water temperature (if a church baptistry) is right, that dressing rooms are ready and that someone is prepared (with extra towels) to assist each candidate out of the water and to the dressing room.

Some words of caution are warranted. Church baptistries pose three serious safety hazards that must be addressed:

**(1) Falls due to wet, slippery surfaces.** A runner of indoor-outdoor carpet from baptistry to dressing room(s) may alleviate this risk.

**(2) Electric shock from microphones or heating elements.** If a portable electric heating element (never recommended) has been used to bring the water up to temperature, disconnect and remove it prior to the ceremony. If a microphone is used for voice amplification, be certain no one in the water touches it under any circumstance—even momentarily.

**(3) Drowning, should children venture too near the water before or after the service.** Assign an usher to see that children do not go near the water. The baptistry should be drained promptly after the service.

Whether the service is specially called or part of one of the regular meetings of the church, it is a sacred occasion. Baptism's potential spiritual impact upon not only the candidates and their relatives but also upon the unbelievers in attendance calls for careful planning and dignified conduct.

Since the ordinance is most commonly included as a part of a regular service, here is a suggested order:

**Hymns:** Sing an appropriate hymn while the minister takes his place in the water.

**Scripture:** The minister reads or quotes one or more of these Scriptures:

And Jesus came and spake unto them, saying, All power is given unto me in heaven and in earth. Go ye therefore, and teach all nations, baptizing them in the name of the Father, and of the Son, and of the Holy Ghost: Teaching them to observe all things whatsoever I have commanded you: and, lo, I am with you alway, even unto the end of the world. Amen.

(Matthew 28:18-20)

And the angel of the Lord spake unto Philip, saying, Arise, and go toward the south unto the way that goeth down from Jerusalem unto Gaza, which is desert. And he arose and went: and, behold, a man of Ethiopia, an eunuch of great authority under Candace queen of the Ethiopians, who had the charge of all her treasure, and had come to Jerusalem for to worship, was returning, and sitting in his chariot read Esaias the prophet. . . . And the eunuch answered Philip, and said, I pray thee, of whom speaketh the prophet this? of himself, or of some other man? Then Philip opened his mouth, and began at the same scripture, and preached unto him Jesus. And as they went on their way, they came unto a certain water: and the eunuch said, See, here is water; what doth hinder me to be baptized? . . . And he commanded the chariot to stand still: and they went down both into the water, both Philip and the eunuch; and he baptized him.

(Acts 8:26-28; 34-36, 38)

What shall we say then? Shall we continue in sin, that grace may abound? God forbid. How shall we, that are dead to sin, live any longer therein? Know ye not, that so many of us as were baptized into Jesus Christ were baptized into his death? Therefore we are buried with him by baptism into death: that like as Christ was raised up from the dead by the glory of the Father, even so we also should walk in newness of life. For if we have been planted together in the likeness of his death, we shall be also in the likeness of his resurrection: Knowing this, that our old man is crucified with him, that the body of sin might be destroyed, that henceforth we should not serve sin. For he that is dead is freed from sin.

(Romans 6:1-7)

**Meditation:** The pastor follows with a brief meditation on the significance of baptism and the occasion at hand.

**Candidate interviews:** As the candidates in turn enter the water, the pastor formally addresses each one with these questions:

**Pastor:** Do you know that you are God's child through faith in the Lord Jesus Christ as your personal Savior?

**Response:** I do.

**Pastor:** Is it your earnest desire to follow Christ in death to self and to walk with Him in newness of life?

**Response:** It is.

**Pastor:** Do you hereby renounce, repudiate and reject the kingdom of darkness, Satan and all his works with all his pomp and pride?

**Response:** I do.

**Testimony:** He invites the candidate to share a brief testimony (prepared beforehand) with the congregation.

**Baptism:** Positioning the folded handkerchief firmly over the candidate's nose and mouth, making sure the candidate is grasping the minister's wrist with both hands, the minister places his left hand below the candidate's shoulders and says:

"_____ [name of candidate], upon your confession of faith in the Lord Jesus Christ as your personal Savior, and by this step of obedience to Him in this ordinance, expressing your desire to follow Him in death to self and to walk with Him in newness of life, I baptize you in the name of the Father, the Son and the Holy Spirit. Amen."

He then briefly immerses the candidate and then helps him or her to exit from the baptistry.

**Hymn or chorus:** During the interval between candidates, a song leader may lead the congregation in a chorus or the verse of a song.

**Fellowship:** Following the service, a time of fellowship to honor the one baptized is an appropriate way to congratulate him on this spiritual milestone.

If the baptism is to be an outdoor service, the above order may be lengthened by extended remarks, congregational singing, special music and longer testimonies by each of the candidates.

At the close of the service, or soon thereafter, the pastor should present properly prepared certificates of baptism to each participant. The church records should also indicate the names of those baptized and the date.

# 5 • Weddings

A WEDDING CEREMONY should be as sacred as communion. Couples should be impressed that it is a covenant between them that God Himself is witnessing. The union of Christ with His Church and the Church's subjection to Him underlie the relationship of marriage and offer the pattern for every godly union. In this day, its sacred character and binding influence must be steadfastly emphasized.

The pastor should ascertain the fitness of the parties to be married, bearing in mind particularly the scriptural restraints on the marriage of divorced persons and believers who would be "yoked together with unbelievers" (2 Corinthians 6:14). Tactfully handled, the act of refusing to perform a marriage ceremony need not prove embarrassing. If the reasons are stated kindly, an opportunity to give spiritual counsel is sometimes afforded. But, embarrassing or not, a minister is under obligation to adhere to the scriptural standards he has pledged to uphold.

Laws governing the performance of the marriage ceremony vary by state and province. The minister should be thoroughly acquainted with the prevailing laws and observe them. Marriages solemnized under circumstances where the minister has failed to comply with such laws are usually considered valid, but the minister himself is subject to censure and possible legal penalty. See that all required reports and forms are filled out properly and promptly. The minister should record each ceremony in the official records of the church. Customarily, he will give a booklet or certificate, inscribed with the facts of the occasion, to the bride and groom.

The minister should arrange a series of premarital conferences with the couple requesting his services. During these conferences, he should discuss the following matters with the couple:

1. The place Christ deserves in the home and the hearts of its occupants; the establishment of a family altar; Sunday observance; regular church attendance.

2. The sacredness of the marriage and its continuing bond.

3. The mutual adjustments necessary for a happy marriage.

4. The preservation in the married life of the love, thoughtfulness and mutual understanding of the courtship.

5. The physical aspects of married life. He may wish either to refer the couple to a Christian medical professional or to competent, well-written books on the subject.

6. Finances, household expenses, savings and monetary support of the church.

7. He will include other matters as experience and discretion dictate. In the case where two unbelievers wish to get married in the church, pastoral sessions should be appropriately adjusted.

It is important to allow ample time for meaningful discussion. Here are some helpful resources for premarital counseling:

· *Called Together* by Steve and Mary Prokopchak, published by Christian Publications, 1999. Based on the principle of lay mentoring within the church, this manual includes segments for both the engaged couple and the mentoring couple. The pastor might use this study as a basis for his own counseling or to initiate the practice of premarital mentoring in his church.

· *The HomeBuilders Video Series* with Dennis Rainey, published by Word Publishing, 1989. This is a six-session marriage enrichment seminar using video tapes, a reproducible study guide and Rainey's book *Staying Close.*

· *The Premarital Counseling Handbook* by H. Norman Wright, published by Moody Press, 1992. This is a major revision of *Premarital Counseling* and includes guidance for holding six counseling sessions.

· *Christian Marital Counseling: Eight Approaches to Helping Couples,* edited by Everett L. Worthington, Jr., published by Baker Books, 1996. This is a good resource for both premarital and marriage counseling.

This chapter contains four sample weddings, a ceremony for renewal of wedding vows and suggestions for a reception. However, it is generally the bride's prerogative to plan the wedding as she wants it. The pastor should go over her plans and wishes thoroughly before the wedding rehearsal. He will be prepared to offer advice whenever it is sought, but he will wisely refrain from proposing changes unless there is some serious infringement on propriety, sanctity of the premises or established local custom. At the rehearsal he will tactfully carry out the bride's plans, even though numerous changes may be proposed by well-meaning friends.

The rehearsal is the time when the participants, including singers, instrumentalist(s) and ushers as well as the wedding party, learn what they are to do and when. If the minister has familiarized himself in advance with the detailed order of the service, as he should, he can be of inestimable help in directing the rehearsal.

Books on etiquette will give ample instruction to the ushers for the proper seating of guests. The processional may vary somewhat, due to the number of attendants, arrangement of the church aisles and plans of the couple. Generally, at a prearranged signal, the minister, groom, best man and ushers will make their appearance in that order, coming in from a side room, and take their places at the altar. The minister will stand in the center and the others at his left, facing the guests. (Sometimes the bride will want the ushers to walk down the aisle with the bridesmaids, or even separately, and take their places at the front.)

Next will come the bridesmaids, maid or matron of honor, ring bearer and/or flower girl(s) and, last, the bride on the left arm of her father or friend. These will take their places at the altar to the right of the minister, the first standing farthest away, the next closer, until finally the bride and her father or friend stand directly in front of the minister.

In most areas, it is customary for the guests to rise at the appearance of the minister or at the entry of the bride. When the bride reaches the altar, the minister will indicate that the guests may be seated.

The order of the recessional is the reverse of the processional. The minister may either walk out with the wedding party as they retire or remain standing at the altar until they exit, after which he retires through the door he entered.

Suggest to the bride that she have the florist arrive two or three hours in advance of the ceremony to do final decorating. This will give the custodian time for final touches to the premises before guests begin to arrive. Also suggest to the bride that no photographs be taken during the ceremony itself. Picture-taking may be tolerated up through the processional and begin again with the recessional, but photographs should not be permitted during the ceremony. Such scenes can be posed afterward.

The minister's poise is the key to a well-regulated wedding ceremony. He should be so familiar with all the particulars that he can impart calmness and inspire confidence. Once the party senses that he is in full command of the situation, they will do their part without mistakes. Should a mistake occur, scarcely anyone will notice it if the minister does not become confused. All he needs to do is give calm instruction or prompting, just as though that was what the ceremony called for, and equilibrium will be maintained.

## A COMPLETE WEDDING CEREMONY

**Minister:** (*Opens the ceremony with Scripture*)

And the LORD God said, It is not good that the man should be alone; I will make him an help meet for him. . . . And the rib, which the LORD God had taken from man, made he a woman, and brought her unto the man. And Adam said, This is now bone of my bones, and flesh of my flesh: she shall be called Woman, because she was taken out of Man. Therefore shall a man leave his father and his mother, and shall cleave unto his wife: and they shall be one flesh.

(Genesis 2:18, 22-24)

Who can find a virtuous woman? for her price is far above rubies. The heart of her husband doth safely trust in her, so that he shall have no need of spoil. She will do him good and not evil all the days of her life.

(Proverbs 31:10-12)

**Minister:** A marriage has always been a joyous occasion. In Cana of Galilee it was gladdened by the presence and blessing of the Lord Jesus Himself. Because God intended marriage to bring blessing and joy to your lives, let us invoke His Presence as you make your covenant before Him and these guests. *(Minister offers a brief invocation.)*

**Minister:** _____ [groom's first name], the Scriptures say to the husband:

Husbands, love your wives, even as Christ also loved the church, and gave himself for it; That he might sanctify and cleanse it with the washing of water by the word, that he might present it to himself a glorious church, not having spot, or wrinkle, or any such thing; but that it should be holy and without blemish. So ought men to love their wives as their own bodies. He that loveth his wife loveth himself.

(Ephesians 5:25-28)

**Minister:** And _____ [bride's first name], the Scriptures say to the wife:

Wives, submit yourselves unto your own husbands, as unto the Lord. For the husband is the head of the wife, even as Christ is the head of the church: and he is the saviour of the body. Therefore as the church is subject unto Christ, so let the wives be to their own husbands in every thing.

(Ephesians 5:22-24)

And to you both, the Scriptures say: "[Submit] yourselves one to another in the fear of God" (Ephesians 5:21).

Marriage was instituted by God Himself, and He performed the first marriage. When a man and a woman have chosen each other and have come to that moment when they sincerely and publicly join in this covenant for life, they lay down on the altar a holy sacrifice to God, to each other and to humanity. The union into which you are now about to enter is the closest and most tender into which human beings can come. It is a union founded upon mutual experience and affection and, to believers in the Lord Jesus Christ, it is a union in the Lord. Marriage is God's institution, intended for the happiness and welfare of humankind.

The Scriptures further say:

> Charity suffereth long, and is kind; charity envieth not; charity vaunteth not itself, is not puffed up, doth not behave itself unseemly, seeketh not her own, is not easily provoked, thinketh no evil; rejoiceth not in iniquity, but rejoiceth in the truth; beareth all things, believeth all things, hopeth all things, endureth all things.

(1 Corinthians 13:4-7)

A union embodying such ideals is not to be entered into lightly or unadvisedly, but reverently, discreetly, soberly and in the fear of

God. Into such a union you come now to be joined.

**Minister:** (*If the bride is to be given in marriage by her father or some other person, the minister will ask the following question.*) Who gives _____ [bride's full name] to be married to _____ [groom's full name]?

**Father or Friend:** I do. (*Or he may say: "Her mother and I."*) (*He will place the bride's hand in the groom's hand and then be seated.*)

**Minister:** (*To the groom*) Before God and these witnesses, will you, _____ [groom's full name], take _____ [bride's full name] to be your wife? Will you love and comfort her, honor and keep her and, in joy and sorrow, preserve with her this bond, holy and unbroken, until the coming of our Lord Jesus Christ, or as long as you both shall live?

**Groom:** I will.

**Minister:** (*To the bride*) Before God and these witnesses, will you, _____ [bride's full name], take _____ [groom's full name] to be your husband? Will you love and comfort him, honor and obey him, keep him in joy and sorrow, preserve with him this bond, holy and unbroken, until the coming of our Lord Jesus Christ, or as long as you both shall live?

**Bride:** I will.

**Groom:** (*Facing his bride and holding her right hand, the man will say his vows either from memory or by following the minister phrase by phrase.*) I, _____ [groom's first name], take you, _____ [bride's first name], to be my wife; to love you with all my heart's affection, to endow you with all my earthly possessions; to give you all the honor of my name; and to share with you the grace of my God.

**Bride:** (*Facing the groom and holding his right hand, the woman shall say her vows either from memory or following the minister phrase by phrase.*) I, _____ [bride's first name], take you, _____ [groom's first name], to be my husband. "Whither thou goest, I will go; and where thou lodgest, I will lodge: thy people shall be my people, and thy God my God" (Ruth 1:16).

**Minister:** As a token of this covenant, you will now give and receive the marriage rings. (*The best man gives the bride's ring to the minister who holds it up for the couple to see.*)

**Minister:** The unbroken circle, the emblem of eternity, and the gold, the emblem of that which is least tarnished and most enduring, are to show how lasting is the pledge you have each made to the other. (*He hands the*

*ring to the groom, who places it on the ring finger
of the bride's left hand.*)

**Minister:** (*The maid or matron of honor gives
the groom's ring to the minister who holds it up for
the couple to see.*) With these emblems of purity and endless devotion, you each the other
wed, and these marriage vows you here and
now forever seal. (*He hands the ring to the bride,
who places it on the ring finger of the groom's left
hand.*)

**Minister:** Let us pray. (*This is the prayer of
dedication. Preferably the couple will kneel and the
minister will place his hands on their shoulders as
he prays. If desired, an appropriate song may precede the prayer.*)

(*Following the prayer, the couple will stand, if
they have been kneeling, and face the minister.*)

**Minister:** Inasmuch as you, _____
[groom's first name], and you, _____
[bride's first name], have thus consented in
holy matrimony and have witnessed the same
before God and these friends, by virtue of the
authority vested in me as a minister of the
Word of God, and by the laws of this state, I
now pronounce you husband and wife. "What
therefore God hath joined together, let not
man put asunder" (Matthew 19:6).

(*The embrace and kiss may follow.*)

**Minister:** Henceforth, you travel life's road together. Let love guide all your relationships. May Christ be the Head of your home, the Unseen Guest at every meal and the Silent Listener to every conversation. May heaven's constant benediction crown your union with increasing joy and blessedness and unite your hearts and lives by the grace and true affection of a happy marriage.

The LORD bless thee, and keep thee: The LORD make his face shine upon thee, and be gracious unto thee: The LORD lift up his countenance upon thee, and give thee peace.

(Numbers 6:24-26)

In the name of the Father, Son and Holy Spirit. Amen!

**Minister:** (*This is the proper place for the pastor to publicly congratulate the couple. As they then turn for the recessional, he may introduce the new bridegroom and bride.*) I present to you Mr. and Mrs. _____ [groom's full name]! (*Or, I present to you [John and Mary Doe]!*)

**Recessional**

## A TRADITIONAL WEDDING CEREMONY

**Minister:** Dearly beloved, we are gathered together here in the sight of God to join together this man and woman in holy matrimony. It is an honorable estate, instituted of God, signifying unto us the mystical union that is between Christ and His Church, that holy estate Christ adorned and beautified with His presence and first miracle in Cana of Galilee. It is commended in the Scriptures to be honorable among all, and therefore is not by any to be entered into unadvisedly or lightly, but reverently, discreetly, advisedly, soberly and in the fear of God. Into this holy estate these two persons present come now to be joined. If any man can show just cause why they may not lawfully be joined together, let him now speak or else hereafter forever hold his peace. (*This is followed by a brief pause.*)

**Minister:** (*To the groom*) _____ [groom's name], wilt thou have this woman to be thy wedded wife, to live together after God's ordinance in the holy estate of matrimony? Wilt thou love her, comfort her, honor and keep her, in sickness and in health, and forsaking others, keep thee only unto her, so long as you both shall live?

**Groom:** I will.

**Minister:** (*To the bride*) _____ [bride's name], wilt thou have this man to be thy wedded husband, to live together after God's ordinance in the holy estate of matrimony? Wilt thou love him, comfort him, honor him, obey him, and keep him, in sickness and in health, and forsaking all others, keep thee only unto him, so long as you both shall live?

**Bride:** I will.

**Minister:** Who giveth this woman to be married to this man?

**Bride's Father (or friend):** I do. (*The father or friend will then place the bride's right hand in the minister's hand. The minister will then place her hand into the groom's right hand.*)

**Minister:** (*To the groom*) Repeat after me. I, _____ [groom's name], take thee, _____ [bride's name], to be my wedded wife, to have and to hold from this day forward, for better, for worse, for richer, for poorer, in sickness and in health, to love and to cherish, till death us do part, according to God's holy ordinance; and thereto do I give thee my pledge.

(*The groom will then release the bride's right hand, and the bride will take the groom's right hand.*)

**Minister:** (*To the bride*) Repeat after me. I, _____ [bride's name], take thee, _____ [groom's name], to be my wedded husband, to have and to hold from this day forward, for better, for worse, for richer, for poorer, in sickness and in health, to love and to cherish, till death us do part, according to God's holy ordinance; and thereto do I give thee my pledge.

(*The two will then release each others' hands.*)

(*At this time, the best man or groom will give the ring to the minister.*)

**Minister:** Bless, O Lord, this ring, that he who gives it and she who wears it may abide in Thy peace and continue in Thy favor, unto their life's end, through Jesus Christ our Lord. Amen.

**Minister:** (*The minister gives the ring to the groom. The groom will take the bride's left hand and place the ring on her third finger, holding it there. The minister speaks to the groom.*) Repeat after me. "With this ring I thee wed, in the name of the Father and of the Son and of the Holy Spirit. Amen."

**Minister:** (*If it is a double-ring ceremony, the maid or matron of honor will give the groom's ring to the minister. The bride will take the groom's left hand and place the ring on his third finger, holding it there. The minister speaks to the bride.*) Repeat after me. "With this ring I thee wed, in the name of the Father and of the Son and of the Holy Spirit. Amen."

(*The couple will release their hands.*)

**Minister:** (*Invites all present to stand and repeat the Lord's Prayer.*)

Our Father which art in heaven, Hallowed be thy name. Thy kingdom come, Thy will be done in earth, as it is in heaven. Give us this day our daily bread. And forgive us our debts, as we forgive our debtors. And lead us not into temptation, but deliver us from evil: For thine is the kingdom, and the power, and the glory, for ever. Amen. (Matthew 6:9-13)

**Minister:** (*The minister will add ONE of the following prayers.*)

O eternal God, Creator and Preserver of all mankind, Giver of all spiritual grace, the Author of everlasting life: Send thy blessing upon these thy servants, this man and this woman, whom we bless in thy name. May they, living faithfully together, perform and keep the vow and covenant between them made, whereof these rings given and received are a token and pledge. May they ever remain in perfect love and peace together, and live according to thy laws, through Jesus Christ our Lord. Amen.

O almighty God, Creator of mankind, who only art the wellspring of life: Bestow upon these thy servants, if it be thy will, the gift and heritage of children; and grant that they may see their children brought up in thy faith and fear, to the honor and glory of thy name, through Jesus Christ our Lord. Amen.

O God, who hast so consecrated the state of matrimony that in it is represented the spiritual marriage and unity between Christ and His church: Look mercifully upon these thy servants. May they love, honor and cherish each other, and so live together in faithfulness and patience, in wisdom and true godliness, that their home may be a haven of blessing and of peace. We pray this through the same Jesus Christ our Lord, who liveth and reigneth with thee and the Holy Spirit ever, one God, world without end. Amen.

**Minister:** (*The minister will now join the couple's right hands together.*) Those whom God hath joined together, let no man put asunder.

**Minister:** (*To all present*) Forasmuch as _____ [groom's name] and _____ [bride's name] have consented together in holy matrimony and have witnessed the same before God and this company, and thereto have given their pledge, each to the other, and have declared the same by giving and receiving rings, and by joining hands, I pronounce that they are husband and wife, in the name of the Father and of the Son and of the Holy Spirit. Amen.

(*At this point, the couple may embrace and kiss.*)

**Minister:** (*The minister may add this blessing.*) May God the Father, God the Son and God the Holy Spirit bless, preserve and keep you. May the Lord mercifully with His favor look upon you and fill you with all spiritual benediction and grace, that you may so live together in this life, that in the world to come you may have life everlasting. Amen.

### A Contemporary Wedding Ceremony

Prelude
Chiming of the hour
Call to worship
Invocation
Hymn
Charge to the witnesses (optional)

**Minister:** In the beginning God created the heavens and the earth. God saw all that He had made and it was very good. The Lord God said, "It is not good that the man should be alone; I will make him an help meet for him." Then the Lord God made a woman from the rib He had taken out of the man, and He brought her to the man. In that act God Himself performed the first wedding ceremony and set the example for all homes in all times.

We are gathered here today several thousands of generations later to follow the example of our God in joining together a man and a woman. We do not do this just as a legal requirement, but rather as a testimony to all that this couple want to obey and follow God in all that they do. You have been invited here as witnesses of this act of worship that this couple today commit before our God. You have also been summoned here to join in that worship of our Lord and Savior Jesus Christ—the Head of every Christian home.

**Ministry of music**
**Processional**
**Presentation of the bride**

**Minister:** Who presents this woman to be married to this man?

**Father:** Her mother and I do. (*Bride steps to left side of groom and together they advance toward the altar.*)

**Scripture readings:** *The minister shall select one or more of the following Scripture.*

**Minister:** Hear the Word of God:

Now the God of patience and consolation grant you to be likeminded one toward another according to Christ Jesus: That ye may with one mind and one mouth glorify God, even the Father of our Lord Jesus Christ. Wherefore receive ye one another, as Christ also received us to the glory of God.

(Romans 15:5-7)

Be kindly affectioned one to another with brotherly love; in honour preferring one another.

(Romans 12:10)

Fulfil ye my joy, that ye be likeminded, having the same love, being of one accord, of one mind. Let nothing be done through strife or vainglory; but in lowliness of mind let each esteem other better than themselves.

(Philippians 2:2-3)

Wives, submit yourselves unto your own husbands, as it is fit in the Lord.

Husbands, love your wives, and be not bitter against them.

(Colossians 3:18-19)

And be ye kind one to another, tender-hearted, forgiving one another, even as God for Christ's sake hath forgiven you.

(Ephesians 4:32)

Forbearing one another, and forgiving one another, if any man have a quarrel against any: even as Christ forgave you, so also do ye. And above all these things put on charity, which is the bond of perfectness. And let the peace of God rule in your hearts, to the which also ye are called in one body; and be ye thankful.

(Colossians 3:13-15)

With all lowliness and meekness, with longsuffering, forbearing one another in love; endeavoring to keep the unity of the Spirit in the bond of peace.

(Ephesians 4:2-3)

That Christ may dwell in your hearts by faith; that ye, being rooted and grounded in love, may be able to comprehend with all saints what is the breadth, and length, and depth, and height; and to know the love of Christ, which passeth knowledge, that ye might be filled with all the fulness of God.

(Ephesians 3:17-19)

Let all bitterness, and wrath, and anger, and clamour, and evil speaking, be put away from you, with all malice.

(Ephesians 4:31)

Charity suffereth long, and is kind; charity envieth not; charity vaunteth not itself, is not puffed up, doth not behave itself unseemly, seeketh not her own, is not easily provoked, thinketh no evil; rejoiceth not in iniquity, but rejoiceth in the truth; beareth all things, believeth all things, hopeth all things, endureth all things. Charity never faileth: but whether there be prophecies, they shall fail; whether there be tongues, they shall cease; whether there be knowledge, it shall vanish away.

(1 Corinthians 13:4-8)

My little children, let us not love in word, neither in tongue; but in deed and in truth.

(1 John 3:18)

Likewise, ye wives, be in subjection to your own husbands; that, if any obey not the word, they also may without the word be won by the conversation of the wives; while they behold your chaste conversation coupled with fear. Whose adorning let it not be that outward adorning of plaiting the hair, and of wearing of gold, or of putting on of apparel; but let it be the hidden man of the heart, in that which is not corruptible, even the ornament of a meek and quiet spirit, which is in the sight of God of great price. . . . Likewise, ye husbands, dwell with them according to knowledge, giving honour unto the wife, as unto the weaker vessel, and as being heirs together of the grace of life; that your prayers be not hindered.

(1 Peter 3:1-4, 7)

And above all things have fervent charity among yourselves: for charity shall cover the multitude of sins. Use hospitality one to another without grudging. As every man hath received the gift, even so minister the same one to another, as good stewards of the manifold grace of God.

(1 Peter 4:8-10)

Wives, submit yourselves unto your own husbands, as unto the Lord. For the husband is the head of the wife, even as Christ is the head of the church: and he is the saviour of the body. Therefore as the church is subject unto Christ, so let the wives be to their own husbands in every thing. Husbands, love your wives, even as Christ also loved the church, and gave himself for it; that he might sanctify and cleanse it with the washing of water by the word, that he might present it to himself a glorious church, not having spot, or wrinkle, or any such thing; but that it should be holy and without blemish. So ought men to love their wives as their own bodies. He that loveth his wife loveth himself. For no man ever yet hated his own flesh; but nourisheth and cherisheth it, even as the Lord the church: For we are members of his body, of his flesh, and of his bones. For this cause shall a man leave his father and mother, and shall be joined unto his wife, and they two shall be one flesh. This is a great mystery: but I speak concerning Christ and the church. Nevertheless let every one of you in particular so love his wife even as himself; and the wife see that she reverence her husband.

(Ephesians 5:22-33)

Let the word of Christ dwell in you richly in all wisdom; teaching and admonishing one another in psalms and hymns and spiritual songs, singing with grace in your hearts to the Lord. And whatsoever ye do in word or deed, do all in the name of the Lord Jesus, giving thanks to God and the Father by him.

(Colossians 3:16-17)

**Declaration of intention**

**Minister:** And now before the omniscient God and in the presence of these witnesses, will you _____ [name of groom], take _____ [name of bride] to be your wedded wife? Will you love and comfort her, honor and keep her and in joy or sorrow preserve with her this union, holy and unbroken until the coming of our Lord Jesus Christ or until God by death shall separate you?

**Groom:** I will.

**Minister:** And now before the omniscient God and in the presence of these witnesses, will you _____ [name of bride], take _____ [name of groom] to be your wedded husband? Will you love and comfort him, honor and obey him, keep him and in joy or sorrow preserve with him this union, holy and unbroken until the coming of our Lord Jesus Christ or until God by death shall separate you?

**Bride:** I will.

Charge to the couple
Exchange of vows and rings

**Groom:** I, _____ [groom's name], take you, _____ [bride's name], to be my wedded wife; to love you with all my heart's affection; to endow you with all my earthly possessions; to give you all the honor of my name; and to share with you the grace of my God.

**Bride:** I, _____ [bride's name], take you, _____ [groom's name], to be my wedded husband; where you go, I will go; where you lodge, I will lodge; your people shall be my people, and your God shall be my God.

*or*

**Groom:** I, _____ [groom's name], take you, _____ [bride's name], to be my wedded wife. With deepest joy I receive you into my life that together we may be one. I take you now to have and to hold from this day forward for better, for worse, for richer, for poorer, in sickness and in health, to love and to cherish till death do us part according to God's Holy Word. And hereto I pledge my faithfulness.

**Bride:** I, _____ [bride's name], take you, _____ [groom's name], to be my wedded husband. With deepest joy I receive you into my life that together we may be one. I take you now to have and to hold from this day forward for better, for worse, for richer, for poorer, in sickness and in health, to love, honor and obey, to cherish till death do us part according to God's

Holy Word. And hereto I pledge my faith-fulness.

*or*

**Groom:** I, _____ [groom's name], take you, _____ [bride's name], to be my wed-ded wife, to have and to hold, from this day forward, for better, for worse, for richer, for poorer, in sickness and in health, to love and to cherish, so long as we both shall live, ac-cording to God's Holy Word, and thereto I give you my pledge.

**Bride:** I, _____ [bride's name], take you, _____ [groom's name], to be my wedded husband, to have and to hold, from this day forward, for better, for worse, for richer, for poorer, in sickness and in health, to love and to cherish, to honor and obey, so long as we both shall live, according to God's Holy Word, and thereto I give you my pledge.

**Minister:** _____ [groom's first name], what token do you give in commemoration of your vows? (*Best man gives ring to minister. He presents it to the groom who places it on the bride's left hand.*)

**Minister:** _____ [bride's first name], what token do you give in commemoration of your vows? (*Maid of honor hands the minister the* *ring. He gives it to the bride who places it on the groom's left hand.*)

There are a number of mementoes of your wedding and of this moment: your wedding picture, the certificate, a pressed flower and many others. But these will for the most part be handled fondly only on occasion. But your rings have a special message and will be the one ever-present and ever-seen reminder of this hour. Here is their message:

They are round. The circle is the symbol of eternity. God intends that this union be until death do you part or until Jesus comes. This is an enduring and lasting and eternal union.

They are a design. Be they ornate or plain, the artisan who designed them had a pattern in mind. So God has a design and pattern in mind for your lives. He has led you together and He has a plan for your future days. It is for you to discover that plan and yield to it and live it in response to His direction.

Your rings are made of a precious metal. That metal was made precious by the re-finer's fire. I wish I could promise you all clear skies and smooth roads but that is not realistic. There will be difficult times and tri-als. These are not meant to divide you but to bind you closer together—to refine the relationship and make this union more precious.

The last thought at this moment, but a valid one, is that all things being equal, it is likely that at some distant point, one of you will be taken before the other. At that moment your rings will serve as a reminder of the ecstasy of this moment and all the wonderful things that you will have shared from this moment to that. Wear them as a constant reminder of these vows and this message.

**Groom:** This ring I give to you in token and pledge of our constant faith and abiding love.

**Bride:** This ring I give to you in token and pledge of our constant faith and abiding love.

*or*

**Groom:** With this ring I thee wed. I give you all my earthly possessions which God has given to me. From this moment forward, may this circle of gold which never ends be a symbol of God's constant, unchanging love, which He gave to me, to give to you eternally. This is my pledge to you of my constant faith and abiding love.

**Bride:** With this ring I thee wed. I give you all my earthly possessions which God has given to me. From this moment forward, may this circle of gold which never ends be a symbol of God's constant, unchanging love, which He gave to me, to give to you eternally. This is my pledge to you of my constant faith and abiding love.

**Prayer of blessing**
**Pronouncement of union**

**Minister:** For as much as _____ [groom's name] and _____ [bride's name] have consented in holy wedlock and have witnessed the same before God and these witnesses, have pledged their faith to each other and have declared the same by joining hands, making vows, and by the giving and receiving of a ring, by the power vested in me by God I now pronounce they are husband and wife in the name of the Father, in the name of the Son, and in the name of the Holy Spirit. Whom God has joined together let no man put asunder.

**Service of communion**
**Minister:** The gift of love is God's greatest gift to man. Realizing its value, _____ [groom's name] and _____ [bride's name] have expressed their desire to always share their love in light of and in obedience to

God's love and will to them. As Christ said, "Do this in remembrance of Me," it is altogether fitting that the first act of this couple as husband and wife should be their sharing in the Lord's Supper.

### Lighting of the wedding candle

**Minister:** The individuals who stand before us have become one. They have separated themselves from their respective families and have formed a single new home. As they signify this by the lighting of their wedding candle, may it be that the light of this new family will shine before men so that their Father in heaven will be glorified.

### Act of appreciation

**Minister:** _____ [groom's name] and _____ [bride's name] are thankful to the homes that have nurtured them and have made it possible for them to stand here today and become husband and wife. They here now especially thank their parents for their contributions to their lives. To publicly signify this, each will now give his own parents a red rose, the symbol of nurture and strength. It is _____'s [groom's name] and _____'s [bride's name] prayer that their new home will be able to give to their offspring this same kind of love and nurture.

**Benediction**

## Minister:

The LORD bless thee, and keep thee: The LORD make his face shine upon thee, and be gracious unto thee: The LORD lift up his countenance upon thee, and give thee peace.

(Numbers 6:24-26)

May the grace of the Lord Jesus Christ, and the love of God the Father, and the communion of the Holy Spirit be with you both. Amen.

**Wedding embrace**
**Presentation**

**Minister:** Brethren and friends, with a heart full of hallelujah, I give to you Mr. and Mrs. _____.

**Recessional**

### AN ALTERNATE CONTEMPORARY CEREMONY

Prelude
Seating of guests
Candle lighting
Seating of parents (first the groom's parents, then
the bride's)
Candle lighting by mothers
Processional (enter groom, groomsmen and pas-
tor)
Bridal procession (congregation standing)
Scripture exhortation

But the LORD is in his holy temple:
let all the earth keep silence before him.

(Habakkuk 2:20)

Be still, and know that I am God: I
will be exalted among the heathen, I
will be exalted in the earth.

(Psalm 46:10)

Invocation:

"Faithful Father and loving Lord, You are the
source of love. Please honor us this day with a
deep sense of Your presence presiding over this
ceremony. Keep us sensitive to the wonder of
things which fill our days and give meaning to
life. Through this ceremony, which celebrates
Your gift of love, deepen within each of us the
level of our loving, both for those who are
close to us as well as strangers who need our

concern. I pray especially for Your superinten-
dence and anointing on these two who come
here at this most significant point in their lives.
Be near to them as they pledge before You
their love, commitment and faithfulness. May
their words mean as much to them as they do
to You, Father. Grant to all of us who have
come to show our support and love a full
measure of Your joy as we share in their celebration. In Jesus' name, Amen.

**Minister:** (*To congregation*) Please be seated.

Statement of purpose

**Minister:** The union which we are here
today to witness is the first and oldest rite in
the world. Marriage was instituted by God
Himself and the first marriage was performed
by Him. So significant is marriage that the
Son of God chose to begin His earthly ministry by joining in a wedding celebration with
friends. So it becomes us all to realize the
sanctity of this ceremony.

What each of us is saying by our presence
here is most significant. Although man is fallen
because of sin, marriage is not fallen. It is a
part of man's original relationship to God
which continues to bring happiness and blessing. Each of us, whether married for many

years or only a few, can discover that blessing and happiness in marriage if it is in our heads to beautify the marriage relationship with tenderness, thoughtfulness, patience, kindness and carefulness in the many ways in which we can express self-sacrifice to the other.

It is just such a commitment of self to one another in Christ which God expects each of us to make, and which _____ [groom's name] and _____ [bride's name] will make in the pledges they give today.

### Giving of the bride

**Minister:** Who has prepared this woman, _____ [bride's full name], for marriage and now gives her to be joined to this man?

**Response:** Her mother and I.

### Expression of intent

**Minister:** (*to the groom*) _____ [groom's name], do you take _____ [bride's name] to be your wife, to live together in the holy bond of married love? Do you promise to honor and uphold her and to join with her in making a home that will endure in love and peace? Do you affirm your purpose of a deeper union with her whereby you both will know joy and the fulfillment of love? Do you pledge to her your complete faithfulness through all the changing experiences of life? And, of your own free will, do you now give yourself to her completely— body, mind and soul—that from this day forward you will be hers alone as long as you both live? If so, please respond by saying, "I do."

**Groom:** I do.

**Minister:** (*to the bride*) _____ [bride's name], do you take _____ [groom's name] to be your husband, to live together in the holy bond of married love? Do you promise to honor and uphold him and to join with him in making a home that will endure in love and peace? Do you affirm your purpose of a deeper union with him whereby you both will know joy and the fulfillment of love? Do you pledge to him your complete faithfulness through all the changing experiences of life? And, of your own free will, do you now give yourself to him completely—body, mind and soul—that from this day forward you will be his alone as long as you both live? If so, please respond by saying, "I do."

**Bride:** I do.

**Minister:** (*to the parents*) I would ask the parents of _____ [bride's name] and _____ [groom's name] to stand at this time. Do you at this most significant juncture in the lives of your children now recommit yourselves to their good? Do you covenant to stand faithfully beside them as they begin their lives together? Do you, believing that God's plans for them are best, promise to support them and offer help to them in decisions that both accord with and oppose your judgments? To engage them not only as your children but also as your friends? To pray for them regularly and do everything in your power to encourage and exhort them to remain faithful to God and to each other? If so, please respond by saying, "I do."

**Parents' Response:** I do.

**Minister:** (*to the congregation*) I would at this time ask for the assembly to stand and join in the declaration of intent. Friends and loved ones of _____ [groom's name] and _____ [bride's name], do you at this time commit yourselves to the loving support, nurture and encouragement of this couple? Do you promise to hold them accountable to the vows they will make before God? To remind them of their sacred commitment to one another and assist them as far as it is possible in maintaining a pure and growing relationship? To model before them and thereby encourage them in a healthy and wholesome marriage relationship?

To stand beside them as they fulfill these vows throughout their lifetime together or until the coming of the Lord Jesus Christ? If so, please respond by saying, "I do."

**Congregation:** I do. (*Congregation may be seated.*)

Scripture reading: 1 Corinthians 13:1-13
Charge to the couple

**Minister:** An excellent illustration of your commitment to one another today is found in the Scriptures in Ecclesiastes 4:9-12. (*Read this portion.*)

There is an interesting formation within this passage that you would do well to remember every day of your life and ministry together: The Teacher speaks of the benefit of two joining as one. He speaks of the aspect of work. Regardless of the work you are engaged in—whether it is your vocations, housework, planning for the future, mowing the lawn or raising a family—the return for your labor together will be greater than ever possible by yourselves.

Through your cooperation, God will grant greater fulfillment and greater achievement in your work. This is one blessing of your union in Him.

Next, the Teacher reminds us that in marriage, God is granting you a representative of Himself to each other. In your spouse, you become and you gain a constant help. From this point on, you will not be without an earthly helper, regardless of the situation. When you fall down, you no longer are responsible to pick yourself up alone, but rather, your helper will be there. What might be trying and difficult alone, you will be able to bear because of your new helper.

Next is the aspect of comfort. We all experience times when we need comfort and encouragement. We are at those times unable to bolster ourselves. We need another close by. Today, God is giving you that one—again as a representative of Himself. What you could not do for yourself will now be accomplished and fulfilled in your life because of the gift of your spouse.

We would expect the sermon in this passage to end with a recapitulation of the value of two coming together, but instead of speaking again of the benefit of two, the writer, who is called the Teacher, speaks of a cord of three strands. He puts the capstone on the concept by suggesting that three, not two, are better than one. This teacher introduces a

new kind of mathematics, so that with re-
gards to the marriage relationship, the for-
mula is $1+1=3$! And this is exciting news!
Today as you become one flesh before God,
He joins the relationship. Can you see the importance of what the Scriptures are saying?

What this means, _____ [groom's
name] and _____ [bride's name], is that
through this sacred bond, the potential for
blessing in your daily living is not doubled
but tripled! The one who works gains not one
coworker, but two. The one who has fallen
has help from a team of two. And the comfort
available in your relationship involves not
just your spouse, but the One who is called
the Comforter!

_____ [groom's name] and _____
[bride's name], God has given you life and
made you for Himself. This same Creator
has placed each of you within the circle of
His love. He gave each of you exposure to
the moods and emotions, tastes and feelings that would shape your individual lives.
You have been loved by others, hurt by others, made happy, made sad. Others have
touched your lives through love, hate, care
and neglect and therefore contributed to
who you are under the supervision of God

your Father and His plan for you. Our Creator-Father carefully filtered what He would permit to touch and form your individual lives for His pleasure. And so, you now not only belong to Him, but this moment, in His presence, He gives you to each other! (*Mention spiritual commitment and the importance of knowing Jesus Christ.*)

Today in God's presence, you are to become a family. The scriptural mystery will again be fulfilled: "The two shall become one flesh." What each of you has been individually, you will now become together with Christ as a partner in your marriage. What has touched your lives, what will touch your lives as individuals, will now become part of a new unity. "The two shall become one flesh." The gift of your separate individuality and uniqueness, today you lay aside in order to share with each other.

_____ [groom's name] and _____ [bride's name], today you join together to become a new family. From two, a new unity of three is now created. Love and hate, care and neglect, hurt and healing, happiness and sorrow will all continue to touch your lives. But what you now experience, you experience together as one.

You are one flesh.

The mystery of this miracle is that the One who gave each of you physical life, the One who worked in your lives as individuals, the One who gave you eternal life through Jesus Christ and the One in whose name you are now joined, will continue to walk with you into your life together. You become today one cord of not two, but three strands. Amen.

### Exchange of vows

**Minister:** At this time, you will exchange vows. _____ [groom's name], will you please make your vows to _____ [bride's name] by repeating after me?

_____ [bride's name], on this day and for the rest of my life, this is the meaning of my love for you: With the Lord's help, I promise to be patient and kind with you, never jealous, to have a humble heart, to honor and respect you, to place your needs before my own, to be slow to anger and quick to forgive, to uphold your faith and rejoice in truth, to bear all things with you, to believe in you, supporting you in all you do, to hope with you and to endure with you in faithfulness until we are home. I promise these things in Christ Jesus our Lord.

**Minister:** And now, _____ [bride's name], will you please make your vows to _____ [groom's name] by repeating after me?

_____ [groom's name], on this day and for the rest of my life, this is the meaning of my love for you: With the Lord's help, I promise to be patient and kind with you, never jealous, to have a humble heart, to honor and respect you, to place your needs before my own, to be slow to anger and quick to forgive, to uphold your faith and rejoice in truth, to bear all things with you, to believe in you, supporting you in all you do, to hope with you and to endure with you in faithfulness until we are home. I promise these things in Christ Jesus our Lord.

### Exchange of rings

**Minister:** What tokens do you present as a symbolic confirmation of your promise to each other?

**Bride and Groom:** These rings.

**Minister:** Wedding rings serve as a fitting symbol of the vows you have just spoken. They are the outward and visible sign of an inward and invisible reality—the love that binds your hearts together in God. Of all the parallels that could be drawn, perhaps these are the most compelling:

1) As these rings are of the finest of earth's materials, so your love is rich in its godly composition and spiritual value;

2) As rings seem to have no beginning or end, so they symbolize the perfection of the love of God for which you will strive in your marriage relationship, that also knows no end. Purity and eternity must characterize the love you have for one another and the union into which you are now entering.

_____ [groom's name], please place the ring on _____'s [bride's name] finger and repeat after me: I give you this ring, in token of our marriage vows. May it ever be a symbol of the unbroken bond of our love.

And now, _____ [bride's name], please place the ring on _____'s [groom's name] finger and repeat after me: I give you this ring, in token of our marriage vows. May it ever be a symbol of the unbroken bond of our love.

### Pronouncement of marriage

**Minister:** By the authority vested in me as a representative of the state and a minister of the gospel, and because of the vows made in the presence of these witnesses, it is my joy to pronounce you husband and wife. Mr. and Mrs. _____ [groom's full name], please welcome one another into your newly formed family with a kiss.

**Unity candle:** *(Special music can be presented during both the unity candle and communion.)*
**Special music**
**Communion**
**Prayer of dedication**

### Minister:

I will lift up mine eyes unto the hills, from whence cometh my help. My help cometh from the LORD, which made heaven and earth. He will not suffer thy foot to be moved: he that keepeth thee will not slumber. Behold, he that keepeth Israel shall neither slumber nor sleep. The LORD is thy keeper: the LORD is thy shade upon thy right hand. The sun shall not smite thee by day, nor the moon by night. The LORD shall preserve thee from all evil: he shall preserve thy soul. The LORD shall preserve thy going out and thy coming in from this time forth, and even for evermore.

(Psalm 121)

Introduction of the new couple

**Minister:** Friends and family, I present to you Mr. and Mrs. _____ [groom's name] and _____ [bride's name] _____ [last name]!

Recessional
Postlude

### OUTLINE FOR REHEARSAL AGENDA

1. Introductions
2. Prayer
3. Overview
4. Line up as you will recess
5. Recess
6. Process from after prelude
7. Questions

**Suggested Receiving Line Order:** Mother of Bride, Mother of Groom, Father of Groom, Father of Bride, Bride, Groom, Maid of Honor, Bridesmaids, Best Man, Groomsmen

### RENEWAL OF VOWS

Light candles
Prelude
**Pastor enters** *(Congregation rises)*
**Processional: Family enters, stands at floor level. Congregation is seated.**

**Minister:** We are gathered together here in the presence of this company to rejoice with this man and this woman on this occasion, and to join with them in the renewal of their marriage vows. They stand before us as an example of the blessedness of matrimony, which St. Paul commended as honorable among all men, and therefore not by any to be entered into unadvisedly or lightly, but reverently, discreetly and in the fear of God.

Congregational hymn: "Amazing Grace"

**Minister:** Now, in the presence of our Lord Jesus Christ, who has led them through many experiences of both joy and difficulty, they give again to each other their hearts, their hands and all that they have and are. (*Couple mounts platform.*)

Renewal of vows

**Minister:** (*to the husband*) _____ [husband's name], in Ephesians 5:25-29 we read:

Husbands, love your wives, even as Christ also loved the church, and gave himself for it; that he might sanctify and cleanse it with the washing of water by the word, that he might present it to himself a glorious church, not having spot, or wrinkle, or any such thing; but that it should be holy and without blemish. So ought men to love their wives as their own bodies. He that loveth his wife loveth himself. For no man ever yet hated his own flesh; but nourisheth and cherisheth it, even as the Lord the church.

_____ [husband's name], nearly ____ years ago, you pledged your loyalty to _____ [wife's name] as your wedded wife. In the presence of God, in the presence of your family and in the presence of these friends who have gathered for this happy occasion, will you now recommit yourself to live with _____ [wife's name] after God's ordinance, in the holy estate of matrimony? Do you promise to love her, comfort her, honor and keep her, in sickness and in health? Will you vow that, forsaking all others, you will keep yourself only unto her, so long as you both should live?

**Husband:** I will.

**Minister:** (*to the wife*) In Ephesians 5:22-24 we are told:

Wives, submit yourselves unto your own husbands, as unto the Lord. For the husband is the head of the wife, even as Christ is the head of the church: and he is the saviour of the body. Therefore as the church is subject to Christ, so let the wives be to their own husbands in every thing.

_____ [wife's name], nearly _____ years ago, you pledged your loyalty to _____ [husband's name] as your wedded husband. In the presence of God, in the presence of your family and in the presence of these friends who have gathered for this happy occasion, will you now recommit yourself to live with _____ [husband's name] after God's ordinance, in the holy estate of matrimony? Do you promise to love him, comfort him, honor and obey him, in sickness and in health? Will you vow that, forsaking all others, you will keep yourself only unto him, so long as you both should live?

**Wife:** I will.

(*Wedding party is seated.*)

**Special music**
**Presentation of token**

*(The man may give to the woman a ring or some other agreed upon token. The man, holding the woman by the hand, shall repeat after the minister.)*

**Minister:** With the giving of this token I renew my vow of love and loyalty. With sincere affection and with all my worldly goods, I continue to thee endow. In the name of the Father and of the Son and of the Holy Ghost. Amen.

*(The woman may give to the man a suitable token. The woman, taking the man by the hand, shall repeat after the minister.)*

**Minister:** With the giving of this token I renew my vow of love and devotion. With sincere affection and with all my worldly goods I continue to thee endow. In the name of the Father and of the Son and of the Holy Ghost. Amen.

**Scripture:** *(The couple may read responsively First Corinthians 13.)*

*or*

*(The couple may wish to read the following reading based on First Corinthians 13.)*

### A Love Pact

**Husband:** I am patient with you because I love you.

I will treat you kindly and never be jealous.

I will not allow boastfulness or pride to interfere with our love.

**Wife:** I will be considerate toward you and seek to fulfill your interest above my own.

I will avoid being angry with you and keep no record of wrongs.

**Husband:** I will take no pleasure in anything that hurts you, but rejoice when you are honored or acknowledged.

I will protect you, trust you and hope the best for you.

**Wife:** My love for you will persevere and, with God's help, it will never fail.

**Unity candle:** (*The organist should play while the candle is being lit.*)

**Minister:** The lighting of the unity candle symbolizes the union of these two individuals joining their lives to form one. May the light of the Lord Jesus shine through them as a couple!

Pronouncement

**Minister:** (*To the guests*) For as much as _____ [full name of husband] and _____ [full name of wife] have consented together in the renewal of their marriage vows, and have witnessed the same before God and this company, and thereto have pledged their faith each to the other by giving and receiving a token, and by joining their hands, I now pray God's richest blessings and richest benediction upon them during the rest of their days as husband and wife together; in the name of the Father and of the Son and of the Holy Ghost. Amen.

**The kiss**

**Minister:**_____ [husband's name], you may kiss your wife.

**Special music**
**Prayer and benediction**
*(Often a receiving line will follow and refreshments will be served.)*

## SUGGESTIONS FOR A CHRISTIAN WEDDING RECEPTION

Every culture has traditions and customs interspersed within it. This is especially true of times relating to special occasions such as weddings. Anyone who has been in our society knows what an ordinary wedding reception entails. The Christian bride and groom should look at the purpose of the after-service gathering and consider making their reception more than ordinary, to elevate it from a mere party to the status of Christian fellowship.

The following are practical ideas which may help in planning for a reception. Please do not dismiss them simply because they are different. Think about these as real possibilities and pray about which ones may apply to you.

1. The place of the reception should be carefully thought through. Often people think only of the location and cost of the place. It is wise, however, to also check the ventilation to be sure there is adequate heat or air-conditioning. Be sure the place is kept clean and that the rest rooms are sufficient for your guests.

2. If a meal is offered be sure it is a quality meal. Be aware that people have a variety of tastes and that medical needs may bring some additional limitations.

3. It is usually a good idea to offer such things as coffee, tea, soft drinks and milk throughout the reception, but one need not offer any intoxicating beverages. These are out of place at a Christian ceremony (see Proverbs 20:1).

4. No wedding is harmed by eliminating dancing. Since it is offensive to many and is often the doorway through which sensuality enters, dancing should be resolutely resisted. A creative couple can have numerous activities which are both fun and consistent with the atmosphere of a family-style celebration. Here are some suggestions:

· **Try a mini-concert.** Many churches have fine musicians, soloists, quartets and ensembles. These people may offer thirty to forty minutes of excellent ministry. Even within the extended family on both sides there may be enough musical and other talent to provide a one-of-a-kind concert for all to enjoy.

· **Try a sing-a-long.** With a good accompanist and song leader this can be most enjoyable. An overhead projector may be used so everyone can know the words.

· **The bride and groom could write letters to their parents and families and then either read them** themselves or have the best man or minister read them. These would be sincere notes of appreciation for the care received in sickness and the hours of overtime put in at the plant. If done with love, and with sufficient effort, this can be a high point that will be remembered by many people for years.

· Try a "roast." Care should be taken so as not to have any hurt feelings, but many will enjoy laughing over childhood remembrances—the first time little Sally made cookies, or those times when Johnny helped Dad fix the car. This may run more smoothly if the thoughts are put together and related by one person. It may also be interesting to hear the first impression the bride and groom had when they met one another.

· Try a version of "The Newlywed Game." Include the couple and perhaps their parents and other family or friends.

5. A word must be given about the garter tradition. It is fun to guess who may be the next ones to be married, but the removal and donning of the garter may prove embarrassing. This can be avoided by having an extra bouquet and garter for the bride and groom to throw. Have those who catch them be congratulated by the wedding couple or offer some special congratulations or hope for the couple.

There will be some people who will consider the above ideas unnecessary, or even prudish, but it should be remembered that the celebration began with the words "Dearly beloved we are gathered together here *in the sight of God.*" Although many will have opinions and try to force their wishes upon the couple, encourage the bride and groom to make their celebration pleasing to the One who began the whole institution of marriage.

# 6 • Funerals

NO DEMAND UPON A PASTOR is greater than the call to minister in the hour of bereavement and death. Never do his people need him more or lean upon him so heavily as then. Nor does the door ever swing so widely to admit him into their hearts' affection and lasting memory as when he comes to minister to them in their time of loss.

Most pastors know when their members may be near death, apart from accidents or a sudden, unexpected passing, and are there to comfort both the dying and those for whom the loss is greatest. But should the pastor, for whatever reason, not be present at the moment, he should go to the sorrowing ones as quickly as possible after the word reaches him. People of his congregation should also be made aware of the death in order that they may offer Christian consolation, perform some thoughtful ministry and attend the funeral service.

At a convenient moment the pastor should ascertain the wishes of the family concerning funeral arrangements. These plans should be followed as closely as possible, although he may tactfully suggest helpful changes. Many will have no idea of how a funeral service is conducted and will appreciate guidance. In other cases, the family may have very definite plans, sometimes prepared by the deceased himself. Such plans should be followed as closely as possible, though if any parts be in conflict with Christian convictions and practice, necessary changes will need to be tactfully suggested. Often a family will desire to prepare a tribute or eulogy, though in many instances the pastor may be requested to write such from information provided.

The congregation should be informed of the death as soon as possible so that they may offer Christian consolation and perform loving ministries, such as the provision of food for the family and the oversight of a fellowship time following the interment, if such is the local custom. Congregational members also need to know so that they may provide support by attendance at the funeral service.

The funeral director generally contacts the minister to determine that plans for the service are fully understood by both. It is not the director's prerogative to alter the plans or say how the service should be conducted. The pastor is responsible for this and will inform the director how the service is to proceed. If the assistance of another minister or the participation of an organization is to be included, such arrangements as are necessary should be made with them.

The pastor's attire should be appropriate, his decorum dignified. He may feel free to speak of the deceased's life and relationship to the church and community, if circumstances seem to warrant it. If he is not entirely familiar with the deceased, he should interview members of the family preferably prior to the family's first visit to the funeral home. Exaggerated eulogies are in poor taste.

In cases where the spiritual condition of the deceased is not known, or his salvation uncertain, it is best to refrain from any reference to that aspect of the life. Do not give empty, false assurances or pass judgment on a person's eternal destiny when not sure of the person's relationship to Christ.

The message should be simple and brief, containing solace for the sorrowing, salvation for the sinner and a glorious hope for all in Christ. A deliberate play upon the emotions is unpardonable. Doctrinal dissertations or any other devices that might interfere with the Spirit's opportunity to move people to Christ should be avoided.

A funeral is a wonderful opportunity to present the gospel and one which should not be missed, since there is often a tenderness, openness and responsiveness which is unique to the occasion. This does not mean, however, that a heavy-handed "altar-call" approach should be employed, though the type of call described later may well be appropriate in some cases. Be gentle, loving and tactful, but be very clear. Man's sin and need, Christ's provision and the absolute necessity for repentance and the acceptance of Christ's atoning work must be presented.

At the grave the minister should be brief, especially if the weather is inclement. After the benediction, he should take time to clasp the hand of each mourner and speak warm words of comfort and encouragement. The pastor will want to visit the mourners in their home or homes within a day or two after the interment to further minister comfort to them. If the deceased was a member or adherent of the church, a suitable word in the church bulletin is appropriate.

An honorarium received for a funeral service should be acknowledged by a gracious letter of thanks and appreciation for the thoughtfulness. Some pastors feel that such an honorarium from members or regular attendants of the church should be returned with an acknowledgment note. This should be determined by local conditions and personal conviction.

## *THE FUNERAL SERVICE*

The funeral service, though it has order and dignity, must not lack warmth, comfort and hope. This suggested order may, of course, be altered by additions, deletions or rearrangement.

### *Suggested Service*

Prelude
Opening Scripture Sentence
Invocation or Lord's Prayer
Special music (optional)
Obituary (if used)
Scripture
Prayer
Special music (If only one musical selection is used, this is perhaps the best time for it.)
Sermon
Prayer
Postlude

*At the cemetery:*

Committal (see pp. 118-130)
Benediction

**Opening Scripture sentence:** Give thought to the choice so that it will be appropriate to the needs of the bereaved. It may be well to use a theme for the whole service, such as comfort, faith, hope, strength, heaven, etc. The selections here are but a few of many appropriate ones.

And [God] said, My presence shall go with thee, and I will give thee rest.

(Exodus 33:14)

Let me die the death of the righteous,
and let my last end be like his!

(Numbers 23:10)

Know therefore that the LORD thy
God, he is God, the faithful God, which
keepeth covenant and mercy with them
that love him and keep his commandments to a thousand generations.

(Deuteronomy 7:9)

The eternal God is thy refuge, and
underneath are the everlasting arms.

(Deuteronomy 33:27)

The LORD gave, and the LORD hath
taken away; blessed be the name of the
LORD.

( Job 1:21)

Though he slay me, yet will I trust in him.

( Job 13:15)

For I know that my redeemer liveth,
and that he shall stand at the latter day
upon the earth. . . . Whom I shall see
for myself, and mine eyes shall behold,
and not another.

(Job 19:25, 27)

God is our refuge and strength, a very present help in trouble.

(Psalm 46:1)

The name of the LORD is a strong tower: the righteous runneth into it, and is safe.

(Proverbs 18:10)

LORD, thou hast been our dwelling-place in all generations. Before the mountains were brought forth, or ever thou hadst formed the earth and the world, even from everlasting to ever-lasting, thou art God.

(Psalm 90:1-2)

Behold, God is my salvation; I will trust, and not be afraid: for the LORD JEHOVAH is my strength and my song; he also is become my salvation.

(Isaiah 12:2)

Thou wilt keep him in perfect peace, whose mind is stayed on thee: because he trusteth in thee. Trust ye in the LORD for ever: for in the LORD JEHOVAH is everlasting strength.

(Isaiah 26:3-4)

Thine eyes shall see the king in his beauty: they shall behold the land that is very far off.

(Isaiah 33:17)

He shall feed his flock like a shepherd: he shall gather the lambs with his arm, and carry them in his bosom.

(Isaiah 40:11)

Fear thou not; for I am with thee: be not dismayed; for I am thy God: I will strengthen thee; yea, I will help thee; yea, I will uphold thee with the right hand of my righteousness.

(Isaiah 41:10)

When thou passest through the waters, I will be with thee; and through the rivers, they shall not overflow thee: when thou walkest through the fire, thou shalt not be burned; neither shall the flame kindle upon thee. For I am the LORD thy God, the Holy One of Israel, thy Saviour.

(Isaiah 43:2-3)

Jesus said unto her, I am the resurrection, and the life: he that believeth in

me, though he were dead, yet shall he
live: And whosoever liveth and believeth in me shall never die.

(John 11:25-26)

Blessed be God, even the Father of our
Lord Jesus Christ, the Father of mercies,
and the God of all comfort; who
comforteth us in all our tribulation, that
we may be able to comfort them which
are in any trouble, by the comfort where-
with we ourselves are comforted of God.

(2 Corinthians 1:3-4)

I have fought a good fight, I have fin-
ished my course, I have kept the faith:
Henceforth there is laid up for me a
crown of righteousness, which the Lord,
the righteous judge, shall give me at that
day: and not to me only, but unto all
them also that love his appearing.

(2 Timothy 4:7-8)

**Invocation:** This will be a brief prayer spoken in a
clear, natural, well modulated voice. It will encourage
quietness of spirit, the yielding of the heart to the wis-

dom of God, grace for the present hour and a deep sense of God's presence and comfort in the service.

**Special music:** The minister is often asked to secure musicians for the service or to include a certain favorite hymn to be sung by a friend. In the absence of musicians, the pastor may read the strengthening words of a stately hymn or a poem of good taste and comfort.

**Obituary or Tribute:** In some cases, unfortunately, this feature of the service has all but disappeared. Where it is used it serves as a general résumé and sometimes eulogy of the deceased. While it is the family's prerogative to choose whether there is to be an obituary/tribute, it may be wise to suggest one.

There is usually great value in an appropriate reference to the life and ministry of the deceased, one which often provides additional comfort to the family and can be enormously healing for the bereaved. This is so whether the family actually prepares the tribute or has someone else do it.

If the pastor is asked to perform this task, it is wise not only to obtain facts, but if possible to sit in on a period of family reminiscences pertaining to the deceased. If the family provides an obituary, it should certainly be used, though it may be edited for sake of clarity.

**Scripture:** The Scripture should be read slowly, distinctly and firmly. As suggested above, it may be the foundation of the funeral sermon. One or more of the following may be used.

**General:**

The LORD is my light and my salvation; whom shall I fear? the LORD is the strength of my life; of whom shall I be afraid? . . . One thing have I desired of the LORD, that will I seek after; that I may dwell in the house of the LORD all the days of my life, to behold the beauty of the LORD, and to enquire in his temple. For in the time of trouble he shall hide me in his pavilion: in the secret of his tabernacle shall he hide me; he shall set me up upon a rock. And now shall mine head be lifted up above mine enemies round about me: therefore will I offer in his tabernacle sacrifices of joy; I will sing, yea, I will sing praises unto the LORD. Hear, O LORD, when I cry with my voice: have mercy also upon me, and answer me. When thou saidst, Seek ye my face; my heart said unto thee, Thy face, LORD, will I seek. . . . Wait on the LORD: be of good courage, and he shall strengthen thine heart; wait, I say, on the LORD.

(Psalm 27:1, 4-8, 14)

He that walketh righteously, and speaketh uprightly; he that despiseth the gain of oppressions, that shaketh his hands from holding of bribes, that stoppeth his ears from hearing of blood, and shutteth his eyes from seeing evil; he shall dwell on high: his place of defence shall be the munitions of rocks: bread shall be given him; his waters shall be sure. Thine eyes shall see the king in his beauty: They shall behold the land that is very far off. . . . But there the glorious LORD will be unto us a place of broad rivers and streams; wherein shall go no galley with oars, neither shall gallant ship pass thereby. For the LORD is our judge, the LORD is our lawgiver, the LORD is our king; he will save us. . . . And the inhabitant shall not say, I am sick: the people that dwell therein shall be forgiven their iniquity.

(Isaiah 33:15-17, 21-22, 24)

Hast thou not known? hast thou not heard, that the everlasting God, the LORD, the Creator of the ends of the earth, fainteth not, neither is weary? there is no searching of his understanding. He giveth power to the faint; and to them that have no might he increaseth strength. . . . But they that wait upon the LORD shall renew their strength; they shall mount up with wings as eagles; they shall run, and not be weary; and they shall walk, and not faint.

(Isaiah 40:28-29, 31)

Now this I say, brethren, that flesh and blood cannot inherit the kingdom of God; neither doth corruption inherit incorruption. Behold, I shew you a mystery; we shall not all sleep, but we shall all be changed, in a moment, in the twinkling of an eye, at the last trump: for the trumpet shall sound, and the dead shall be raised incorruptible, and we shall be changed. For this corruptible must put on incorruption, and this mortal must put on immortality. So when this corruptible shall have put on incorruption, and this mortal shall have put on immortality, then shall be brought to pass the saying that is written, Death is swallowed up in victory. O death, where is thy sting? O grave, where is thy victory? The sting of death is sin; and the strength of sin is the law.

But thanks be to God, which giveth us the victory through our Lord Jesus Christ. Therefore, my beloved brethren, be ye stedfast, unmoveable, always abounding in the word of the Lord, forasmuch as ye know that your labour is not in vain in the Lord.

(1 Corinthians 15:50-58)

But I would not have you to be ignorant, brethren, concerning them which are asleep, that ye sorrow not, even as others which have no hope. For if we believe that Jesus died and rose again, even so them also which sleep in Jesus will God bring with him. For this we say unto you by the word of the Lord, that we which are alive and remain unto the coming of the Lord shall not prevent them which are asleep. For the Lord himself shall descend from heaven with a shout, with the voice of the archangel, and with the trump of God: and the dead in Christ shall rise first: Then we which are alive and remain shall be caught up together with them in the clouds, to meet the Lord in the air: and so shall we ever be with the Lord. Wherefore comfort one another with these words.

(1 Thessalonians 4:13-18)

**For a child or young person:**

David therefore besought God for the child; and David fasted, and went in, and lay all night upon the earth. And the elders of his house arose, and went to him, to raise him up from the earth: but he would not, neither did he eat bread with them. And it came to pass on the seventh day, that the child died. And the servants of David feared to tell him that the child was dead: for they said, Behold, while the child was yet alive, we spake unto him, and he would not hearken unto our voice: how will he then vex himself, if we tell him that the child is dead? But when David saw that his servants whispered, David perceived that the child was dead: therefore David said unto his servants, Is the child dead? And they said, He is dead. Then David arose from the earth, and washed, and anointed himself, and changed his apparel, and came into the house of the LORD, and worshipped: then he came to his own house; and when he required, they set bread before him, and he did eat. Then said his servants unto him, What thing is this that thou hast done? thou didst fast and weep for the child, while it was alive; but when the child was dead, thou didst rise and eat bread. And he said, While the child was yet alive, I fasted and wept: for I said, Who can tell whether GOD will be gracious to me, that the child may live? But now he is dead, wherefore should I fast? can I bring him back again? I shall go to him, but he shall not return to me.

(2 Samuel 12:16-23)

The LORD is my shepherd; I shall not want. He maketh me to lie down in green pastures: he leadeth me beside the still waters. He restoreth my soul: he leadeth me in the paths of righteousness for his name's sake. Yea, though I walk through the valley of the shadow of death, I will fear no evil: for thou art with me; thy rod and thy staff they comfort me. Thou preparest a table before me in the presence of mine enemies: thou anointest my head with oil; my cup runneth over. Surely goodness and mercy shall follow me all the days of my life: and I will dwell in the house of the LORD for ever.

(Psalm 23)

And they brought young children to him, that he should touch them: and his disciples rebuked those that brought them. But when Jesus saw it, he was much displeased, and said unto them, Suffer the little children to come unto me, and forbid them not: for of such is the kingdom of God. Verily I say unto you, Whosoever shall not receive the kingdom of God as a little child, he shall not enter therein. And he took them up in his arms, put his hands upon them, and blessed them.

(Mark 10:13-16)

**For the faithful adult:**

Blessed is the man that walketh not in the counsel of the ungodly, nor standeth in the way of sinners, nor sitteth in the seat of the scornful. But his delight is in the law of the LORD; and in his law doth he meditate day and night. And he shall be like a tree planted by the rivers of water, that bringeth forth his fruit in his season; his leaf also shall not wither; and whatsoever he doeth shall prosper. The ungodly are not so: but are like the chaff which the wind driveth away. Therefore the ungodly shall not stand in the judgment, nor sinners in the congregation of the righteous. For the LORD knoweth the way of the righteous: but the way of the ungodly shall perish.

(Psalm 1)

LORD, who shall abide in thy tabernacle? who shall dwell in thy holy hill? He that walketh uprightly, and worketh righteousness, and speaketh the truth in his heart. He that backbiteth not with his tongue, nor doeth evil to his neighbour, nor taketh up a reproach against his neighbour. In whose eyes a vile person is contemned; but he honoureth them that fear the LORD. He that sweareth to his own hurt, and changeth not. He that putteth not out his money to usury, nor taketh reward against the innocent. He that doeth these things shall never be moved.

(Psalm 15)

Who can find a virtuous woman? for her price is far above rubies. The heart of her husband doth safely trust in her, so that he shall have no need of spoil. She will do him good and not evil all the days of her life. . . . She stretcheth out her hand to the poor; yea, she reacheth forth her hands to the needy. . . . Strength and honour are her clothing; and she shall rejoice in time to come. She openeth her mouth with wisdom; and in her tongue is the law of kindness. She looketh well to the ways of her household, and eateth not the bread of idleness. Her children arise up, and call her blessed; her husband also, and he praiseth her. Many daughters have done virtuously, but thou excellest them all. Favour is deceitful, and beauty is vain: but a woman that feareth the LORD, she shall be praised.

Give her the fruit of her hands; and let
her own works praise her in the gates.

(Proverbs 31:10-12, 20, 25-31)

Let not your heart be troubled: ye believe in God, believe also in me. In my
Father's house are many mansions: if it
were not so, I would have told you. I go
to prepare a place for you. And if I go
and prepare a place for you, I will come
again, and receive you unto myself; that
where I am, there ye may be also. And
whither I go ye know, and the way ye
know. Thomas saith unto him, Lord,
we know not whither thou goest; and
how can we know the way? Jesus saith
unto him, I am the way, the truth, and
the life: no man cometh unto the Father, but by me. . . . Peace I leave with
you, my peace I give unto you: not as
the world giveth, give I unto you. Let
not your heart be troubled, neither let it
be afraid.

(John 14:1-6, 27)

Blessed be the God and Father of our
Lord Jesus Christ, which according to his

abundant mercy hath begotten us again unto a lively hope by the resurrection of Jesus Christ from the dead, to an inheritance incorruptible, and undefiled, and that fadeth not away, reserved in heaven for you, who are kept by the power of God through faith unto salvation ready to be revealed in the last time. Wherein ye greatly rejoice, though now for a season, if need be, ye are in heaviness through manifold temptations: That the trial of your faith, being much more precious than of gold that perisheth, though it be tried with fire, might be found unto praise and honour and glory at the appearing of Jesus Christ: Whom having not seen, ye love; in whom, though now ye see him not; yet believing, ye rejoice with joy unspeakable and full of glory: Receiving the end of your faith, even the salvation of your souls.

(1 Peter 1:3-9)

**For the elderly person:**

LORD, thou hast been our dwelling-place in all generations. Before the mountains were brought forth, or ever thou hadst formed the earth and the world, even from everlasting to everlasting, thou art God. Thou turnest man to destruction; and sayest, Return, ye children of men. For a thousand years in thy sight are but as yesterday when it is past, and as a watch in the night. Thou carriest them away as with a flood; they are as a sleep: in the morning they are like grass which groweth up. In the morning if flourisheth, and groweth up; in the evening it is cut down, and withereth. . . . For all our days are passed away in thy wrath: we spend our years as a tale that is told. The days of our years are threescore years and ten; and if by reason of strength they be fourscore years, yet is their strength labour and sorrow; for it is soon cut off, and we fly away. . . . So teach us to number our days, that we may apply our hearts unto wisdom.

(Psalm 90:1-6, 9-10, 12)

He that dwelleth in the secret place of the most High shall abide under the shadow of the Almighty. I will say of the LORD, He is my refuge and my fortress: my God; in him will I trust. Surely he will deliver thee from the snare of the fowler, and from the noisome pestilence. He shall cover thee with his feathers, and under his wings shalt thou trust: his truth shall be thy shield and buckler.

(Psalm 91:1-4)

And I saw a new heaven and a new earth: for the first heaven and the first earth were passed away; and there was no more sea. And I John saw the holy city, new Jerusalem, coming down from God out of heaven, prepared as a bride adorned for her husband. And I heard a great voice out of heaven saying, Behold, the tabernacle of God is with men, and he will dwell with them, and they shall be his people, and God himself shall be with them, and be their God. And God shall wipe away all tears from their eyes; and there shall be no more death, neither sorrow, nor crying, neither shall there be any more pain: for the former things are passed away. And he that sat upon the throne said, Behold, I make all things new. And he said unto me, Write: for these words are true and faithful. And he said unto me, It is done. I am Alpha and Omega, the beginning and the end. I will give unto him that is athirst of the fountain of the water of life freely. He that overcometh shall inherit all things; and I will be his God, and he shall be my son.

(Revelation 21:1-7)

And he shewed me a pure river of water of life, clear as crystal, proceeding out of the throne of God and of the Lamb. In the midst of the street of it, and on either side of the river, was there the tree of life, which bare twelve manner of fruits, and yielded her fruit every month: and the leaves of the tree were for the healing of the nations. And there shall be no more curse: but the throne of God and of the Lamb shall be in it; and his servants shall serve him: And they shall see his face; and his name shall be in their foreheads. And there shall be no night there; and they need no candle, neither light of the sun; for the Lord God giveth them light: and they shall reign for ever and ever.

(Revelation 22:1-5)

**For the unbeliever:**

To every thing there is a season, and a time to every purpose under the heaven: A time to be born, and a time to die; a time to plant, and a time to pluck up that which is planted; a time to kill, and a time to heal; a time to break down, and a time to build up; a time to weep, and a time to laugh; a time to mourn, and a time to dance; a time to cast away stones, and a time to gather stones together; a time to embrace, and a time to refrain from embracing; a time to get, and a time to lose; a time to keep, and a time to cast away; a time to rend, and a time to sew; a time to keep silence, and a time to speak; a time to love, and a time to hate; a time of war, and a time of peace. What profit hath he that worketh in that wherein he laboureth? I have seen the travail, which God hath given to the sons of men to be exercised in it. He hath made every thing beautiful in his time: also he hath set the world in their heart, so that no man can find out the work that God maketh from the beginning to the end. I know that there is no good in them, but for a man to rejoice, and to do good in his life. And also that every man should eat and drink, and enjoy the good of all his labour, it is the gift of God. I know that, whatsoever God doeth, it shall be for ever: nothing can be put to it, nor any thing taken from it: and God doeth it, that men should fear before him. That which hath been is now; and that which is to be hath already been; and God requireth that which is past.

(Ecclesiastes 3:1-15)

The days of our years are threescore years and ten; and if by reason of strength they be fourscore years, yet is their strength labour and sorrow; for it is soon cut off, and we fly away. . . . So teach us to number our days, that we may apply our hearts unto wisdom. . . .

O satisfy us early with thy mercy; that we may rejoice and be glad all our days. Make us glad according to the days wherein thou hast afflicted us, and the years wherein we have seen evil. Let thy work appear unto thy servants, and thy glory unto their children. And let the beauty of the LORD our God be upon us: and establish thou the work of our hands upon us; yea, the work of our hands establish thou it.

(Psalm 90:10, 12, 14-17)

Go to now, ye that say, To day or to morrow we will go into such a city, and continue there a year, and buy and sell, and get gain: Whereas ye know not what shall be on the morrow. For what is your life? It is even a vapour, that appeareth for a little time, and then vanisheth away. For that ye ought to say, If the Lord will, we shall live, and do this, or that. But now ye rejoice in your boastings: all such rejoicing is evil.

(James 4:13-16)

**Prayer:** The prayer should be a simple, heartfelt petition on behalf of those who sorrow. If they are members of the church or well-known friends, it may be appropriate to pray for them by name. Obviously, if the petition is that any who know not Christ be led to prepare for their own meeting with God, it is not appropriate to name such ones.

**Sermon:** Most of the suggested Scriptures above could be the basis for the pastor's message to the bereaved. The message itself will always be brief, simple and comforting, never delivered in harsh or loud tones, always directed to the living and not to the dead. Let there be abundant expressions of comfort—an assignment not difficult if the deceased is a believer.

The message should also point the way to salvation. Seldom will the minister have a funeral when *everyone* in attendance is a believer. Occasionally the minister is asked by the family to invite those in attendance to respond publicly following his message. He will explain the request and extend the invitation as simply and appropriately as possible. It is hardly wise to ask people to move forward around the casket. But he can ask people to stand or to raise their hands in response. As soon as possible, he will want to contact them to confirm their decision. But whether a public profession is included or not, the message should point up the need for a personal experience of faith.

**Prayer:** This prayer following the sermon will be brief, asking that the sorrowing might be enabled to direct their hearts and hopes to the Word just set before them, finding its strength and solace for their need now and in days to come.

If the burial will be at a distant place where most of those present at the funeral will not attend, the minister should here read an appropriate selection from the committal liturgy and conclude with this sentence:

"We now commit the body of this loved one and friend to those who will convey it to another community, there to be laid to rest until God calls it to resurrection."

**Benediction:** The benediction will follow the prayer above if interment is to be local and attended by most of those present. Otherwise it will follow the committal sentence above.

At this point, the funeral director takes charge. If there is to be a final viewing of the body, he or she will direct this, as well as the departure from the building to the funeral procession. The minister waits in the place indicated until the casket is in readiness to be taken to the funeral car. He will precede the pallbearers and the casket. From here, he will go to the car that is to convey him to the cemetery.

## THE COMMITTAL SERVICE

At the cemetery, the minister will proceed slowly ahead of the casket to the grave, where he will stand at the end or to the rear until all have assembled. The funeral director will signal him when he is to begin. The pastor may select from the following committals or prepare one of his own.

**General:** This first committal service requires that the pastor have a rose and a bit of evergreen in hand. The funeral director will provide such, if requested in advance.

**Minister:** Friends, we are gathered at the final resting place of all that is mortal of _____ [the full name of the deceased].

Brother [or sister], we spread symbolically over your body the garments of nature and tuck them securely in: the delicate shades of spring; the green of summer; the gold of autumn; and the spotless white of winter. Your memory is to your loved ones, and to us, as fragrant as the rose [*place the rose on the casket*], and as lasting as the evergreen [*place evergreen*]. Rest in peace upon the bosom of your Lord.

And so, until the day dawns and the shadows flee away and all who know the Lord meet again in the full glory of the resurrection morning, we bid you not good-bye, but just good night!

*(Please note: This committal is not suitable for use if there is a question as to the spiritual condition of the deceased.)*

For a believer:

**Minister:** (*Begins with this scripture*)

But I would not have you to be ignorant, brethren, concerning them which are asleep, that ye sorrow not, even as others which have no hope. For if we believe that Jesus died and rose again, even so them also which sleep in Jesus will God bring with him. For this we say unto you by the word of the Lord, that we which are alive and remain unto the coming of the Lord shall not prevent them which are asleep. For the Lord himself shall descend from heaven with a shout, with the voice of the archangel, and with the trump of God: and the dead in Christ shall rise first: Then we which are alive and remain shall be caught up together with them in the clouds, to meet the Lord in the air: and so shall we ever be with the Lord. Wherefore comfort one another with these words.

(1 Thessalonians 4:13-18)

**Minister:** We gather here to commit to this resting place the body of our loved one and friend, whose spirit is already with the Lord. While this spot of earth will hold the form of one whose memory we shall treasure, we look not here in sorrow as those who have no hope. We believe that to be absent from the body is to be present with the Lord and that to die is gain. We therefore commit this body to the ground in the renewed and fresh hope of the return of Christ, at whose appearing "the dead in [Him] shall rise first: Then we which are alive and remain shall be caught up together with them in the clouds, to meet the Lord in

the air: and so shall we ever be with the Lord"
(1 Thessalonians 4:16-17).

*or*

**Minister:** (*Begin with this text.*)

Behold, I shew you a mystery; we
shall not all sleep, but we shall all be
changed, in a moment, in the twinkling
of an eye, at the last trump: for the
trumpet shall sound, and the dead shall
be raised incorruptible, and we shall be
changed. For this corruptible must put
on incorrup- tion, and this mortal must
put on immortality. So when this corruptible shall have put on incorruption,
and this mortal shall have put on immortality, then shall be brought to pass
the saying that is written, Death is
swallowed up in victory. O death,
where is thy sting? O grave, where is
thy victory? The sting of death is sin;
and the strength of sin is the law. But
thanks be to God, which giveth us the
victory through our Lord Jesus Christ.
Therefore, my beloved brethren, be ye
stedfast, unmoveable, always abounding in the work of the Lord, forasmuch

as ye know that your labour is not in vain for the Lord.

(1 Corinthians 15:51-58)

**Minister:** We have gathered here to commit to this resting place the body of our loved one and friend:

Cherishing memories that are forever
    sacred,
Sustained by a faith that is stronger
    than death,
And comforted by the hope of a life that
    shall endless be,
We commit to the earth all that is
    mortal of this one.

And as we have borne the image of the earthy, we shall also bear the image of the heavenly.

(1 Corinthians 15:49)

*or*

The LORD is my light and my salvation; whom shall I fear? the LORD is the strength of my life; of whom shall I be afraid? . . . One thing have I desired of the LORD, that will I seek after; that I may dwell in the house of the LORD all the days of my life, to behold the beauty of the LORD, and to enquire in his temple.

(Psalm 27:1, 4)

**Minister:** Some of us have shared through these passing years a wonderful companionship and fellowship with our faithful brother [sister]. We cherish the many blessed and hallowed memories that come to us in these moments. His [her] faithfulness, friendship and consecrated life will continue their radiance and testimony in our lives, our church and our community. In the name of Jesus Christ, whom he [she] loved and served, we commit his [her] body to this resting place, knowing that his [her] spirit is with the Lord in His heavenly house. In so doing, we rest our hearts in fresh confidence upon the sure and certain hope of the resurrection to life eternal through Jesus Christ our Lord.

*or*

**Minister:** Hear the comforting words of Scripture:

The LORD gave, and the LORD hath taken away; blessed be the name of the LORD.

(Job 1:21)

Let not your heart be troubled: ye believe in God, believe also in me.

(John 14:1)

Forasmuch as it has pleased Almighty God in His great mercy to take unto Himself the soul of our brother [sister], we therefore commit his [her] body to the ground—earth to earth, ashes to ashes, dust to dust—in the sure and certain hope of the resurrection through "the Lord Jesus Christ: Who shall change our vile body, that it may be fashioned like unto his glorious body, according to the working whereby he is able even to subdue all things unto himself" (Philippians 3:20-21). Amen.

### Committal for a child:

He shall feed his flock like a shepherd: he shall gather the lambs with his arm, and carry them in his bosom, and shall gently lead those that are with young.

(Isaiah 40:11)

Suffer the little children to come unto me, and forbid them not: for of such is the kingdom of God. Verily I say unto you, Whosoever shall not receive the kingdom of God as a little child, he shall not enter therein. And he took them up

in his arms, put his hands upon them,
and blessed them.

(Mark 10:14-16)

Again the arms of our Savior have opened
to a child whom He has clasped to Himself in
tenderest love. He has instructed us to "suffer
the little children to come unto [Him]" not to
"forbid them." The going of this one so dear
to our hearts has brought heaven nearer.

or (using same Scriptures)

"For of such is the kingdom of God" (Mark
10:14). Today we feel that heaven is more
real than ever. As we held this little one, we
held eternity in our arms.

Heed the words of Jesus that instruct us to
"receive the kingdom of God as a little child"
if we are to enter it. Would that all were as
sure of their ultimate place in God's kingdom
as we are of this little one's welcome there.

Being comforted, then, by this truth, we
commit his [her] body to this place of rest.
We here renew our determination to give
heed to our own soul's need, so that we too
may inherit eternal life through Jesus Christ
our Lord.

*or (using same Scriptures)*

The eternal God is thy refuge, and underneath are the everlasting arms.

(Deuteronomy 33:27)

Forasmuch as it has pleased the Heavenly Father and Shepherd of the lambs to take into His eternal fold this child, we therefore commit his [her] body to the ground.

They shall hunger no more, neither thirst any more; neither shall the sun light on them, nor any heat. For the Lamb which is in the midst of the throne shall feed them, and shall lead them unto living fountains of waters: and God shall wipe away all tears from their eyes.

(Revelation 7:16-17)

**For a non-Christian:**

God is our refuge and strength, a very present help in trouble. Therefore will not we fear, though the earth be removed, and though the moutains be carried into the midst of the sea; though the water thereof roar and be troubled, though the mountains shake with the swelling thereof.

(Psalm 46:1-3)

Before the mountains were brought forth, or ever thou hadst formed the earth and the world, even from everlasting to everlasting, thou art God. Thou turnest man to destruction; and sayest, Return, ye children of men. For a thousand years in thy sight are but as yesterday when it is past, and as a watch in the night. Thou carriest them away as with a flood; they are as a sleep: in the morning they are like grass which groweth up. In the morning it flourisheth, and groweth up; in the evening it is cut down, and withereth.

(Psalm 90:1-6)

As for man, his days are as grass: as a flower of the field, so he flourisheth. For the wind passeth over it, and it is gone; and the place thereof shall know it no more.

(Psalm 103:15-16)

Life, at best, is short. We brought nothing into this world, and we can carry nothing out. In the midst of life we are in the midst of death. "And as it is appointed unto men once to die, but after this the judgment" (Hebrews 9:27), let us here purpose to seek the Lord with all our hearts and respond to the opportunities of salvation extended to us through His grace.

The Scriptures say it is "the goodness of God" that "leadeth [us] to repentance" (see Romans 2:4). And repentance leads us to His greatest gift, the gift of eternal life through the Lord Jesus Christ. May each gift of God's kindness remind us of His love toward us in Christ. We commit now the body of this loved one to this resting place; the spirit we leave with God, for "Shall not the Judge of all the earth do right?" (Genesis 18:25).

**Prayer and benediction:** Proceed from the committal to a prayer for the comfort of the sorrowing and for their adjustment and wisdom for the days ahead, concluding with a benediction, such as these that follow.

The LORD bless thee, and keep thee: The LORD make his face shine upon thee, and be gracious unto thee: The LORD lift up his countenance upon thee, and give thee peace.

(Numbers 6:24-26)

And the peace of God, which passeth all understanding, shall keep your hearts and minds through Christ Jesus.

(Philippians 4:7)

Now our Lord Jesus Christ himself, and God, even our Father, which hath loved us, and hath given us everlasting consolation and good hope through grace, comfort your hearts, and stablish you in every good word and work.

(2 Thessalonians 2:16-17)

Now the God of peace, that brought again from the dead our Lord Jesus, that great shepherd of the sheep, through the blood of the everlasting covenant. Make you perfect in every good work to do his will, working in you that which is wellpleasing in his sight, through Jesus Christ; to whom be glory for ever and ever. Amen.

(Hebrews 13:20-21)

The graveside service is frequently the most difficult for the mourners. It is sometimes terrifying for them to think of leaving their loved one there to be buried in the ground, to be seen no more. The minister, therefore, as soon as he concludes the service, should step to the side of the principal mourners to give his personal word of encouragement to them. He may linger with them a moment to be of any assistance that he can, should they be overcome by emotion.

At the conclusion of the service, there is frequently an opportune moment to speak quietly with some individual about his spiritual needs.

# 7 • A Service of Anointing for Healing

CHRIST GAVE HIS CHURCH the ministry of healing. James offers a scriptural basis for such a practice: "Is any sick among you? let him call for the elders of the church; and let them pray over him, anointing him with oil in the name of the Lord: And the prayer of faith shall save the sick, and the Lord shall raise him up" (James 5:14-15).

Here believers have instructions as to what to do in the case of sickness. The suffering believer is to call for the elders of the church. The elders are not only to pray but also to anoint with oil. The oil in Scripture is often a type of the Holy Spirit. It is to be done in Jesus' name, that is, by His authority.

Some churches schedule a time to meet with those who are sick just following the communion service. But because sickness may intrude at any time, the elders may be required to go to the home or to the hospital.

The pastor being the head elder, if available, will lead the prayer engagement. He will ascertain the problem. It may be a need for physical healing, inner healing because of past hurts or spiritual healing because of unconfessed sin. Time should be given for the confession of sin by any and all involved. He will then anoint with oil from a vial of olive oil,* placing a small amount of oil on the forehead of the sick person. The elders will then place their hands on the person while two or three offer a sincere prayer for divine healing of body, soul or spirit, depending on the need. On occasion there may be need for further interviewing.

* Oil vials may be ordered from e-church depot at 1-800-233-4443.

# 8 • Installation Services

## INSTALLATION OF A PASTOR

IN KEEPING WITH THE HOLY solemnity and sacred dignity under which men are set apart for the gospel ministry, it is fitting that a pastor's tenure in a given locale begin in a similar atmosphere.

The responsibility for his installation usually rests with the district superintendent or local ministerium president. He, together with local church leadership, initiates arrangements. If neighboring pastors and representatives from local ministeriums are to be invited to participate, he will see that they are contacted and assigned specific parts in the service. The chairman of the church's governing board or board of elders is generally designated to speak for the church.

The Service of Installation should take place as soon as possible after the new pastor arrives, preferably on the first or second Sunday after his ministry to the new congregation begins. The day and time for the service are largely dictated by area custom.

If the installation is part of a regular service, the usual order of service will prevail, with adjustments suitable to incorporate the essential elements. The following suggested outline is for the preparation of a simple service devoted entirely to the installation:

## *Service of Installation for a Pastor*

*Suggested Service*

Prelude

Welcome by the moderator (District Superintendent or president of local ministerium)

Hymn

Invocation and the Lord's Prayer

Scripture reading (or responsive reading)

Love offering (usually given to the new pastor's
wife for decorating her new home)

Hymn (or worship chorus selections)

Charge to the congregation (by a local pastor or
district official)

Response (by the Chairman of the Governing
Board or Elder Chairman)

Special music

Charge to the Pastor (District Superintendent or
area pastor)

Response (from the new pastor)

Orders of Installation (printed in worship folder
or distributed to congregation and delivered by the
Moderator)

**Moderator:** Pastor, this is a service of personal dedication to your task. During these
sacred moments will you consider anew that
particular call of God that has come to you for
this task, and will you allow God's Holy Spirit
to remind you of the divine resources available to you for your work? Do you sincerely
believe that you have been led by the Spirit of

God to engage in this work and to assume its responsibilities?

**Pastor:** I do so believe.

**Moderator:** In humble reliance upon divine grace, do you make it your aim to give yourself unreservedly to the work of God in this office?

**Pastor:** I do, the Lord being my Helper.

**Moderator:** Do you, the congregation, affirm this leader?

**Congregation in unison:** We do.

**Moderator:** Do you pledge to him your support and prayers?

**Congregation in unison:** We pledge to him our prayers, support and affirmation.

**Prayer of installation** (*All clergy and local church elders gather around the new pastor and his wife for the laying on of hands and a prayer offered by the Moderator or selected individual.*)

**Closing hymn**
**Closing prayer and benediction**
**Postlude**

It is appropriate for the congregation to stand for the hymns, the closing prayer and benediction.

With minor adaptation, the above ceremony can be used for the installation of a member of the pastoral staff as well as for the senior or solo pastor. Depending on local custom, a time of fellowship and refreshments may follow the service.

## INSTALLATION OF CHURCH OFFICERS

No service rendered in the name of the Lord Jesus Christ is small or unimportant. A service of installation, if given proper planning and dignity, will reinforce that conviction for both the church's leadership and membership.

If the minister chooses to preach a sermon on some theme related to office-holding and service, the installation might well follow the message. It is also appropriate to conduct the ceremony prior to the serving of communion or at some other place in the worship order.

The installation ceremony should be conducted during a morning worship service as close as possible to the date the leaders assume office. The pastor will carefully explain the procedure to those involved so that they can fulfill his directions without confusion. If possible, the entire staff of newly elected officers should be present for this occasion. A place is generally reserved for them to sit together near the front of the sanctuary.

All elected and appointed leadership may be installed at one time using one generic ceremony or each grouping of officers (i.e., governing board, elders, deacons, deaconesses, etc.) may be installed separately using a more specifically crafted version of the ceremony suggested below.

### Outline for Installation of Church Officers

**Hymn** ("Take My Life and Let It Be," "Make Me a Blessing," "Channels Only" or "My Trust" or a chorus like "Faithful Men")

**Scripture:** An appropriate Scripture selection such as 1 Timothy 3:1-7 (elders/overseers); 1 Timothy 3:8-13 (deacons); Titus 1:5-9 (elders); 1 Peter 5:2-4 (elders/overseers); or Romans 12:6-18 might be read.

**Presentation of officers:** The officers may be asked to stand where they are or come to the front of the sanctuary. They are then introduced by name by the pastor or by the chairman of their respective committees.

### Statement of duties

**Pastor:** The appointment given you by your fellow members is one that should be entered into with solemnity and faith. We are not sufficient of ourselves for such a responsibility. But God, who has called us, "is able to make all grace abound toward you; that ye, always having all sufficiency in all things, may abound to every good work" (2 Corinthians 9:8).

It is imperative that you guard your behavior and your words. In a special sense, you are examples and models. The measure of your godliness and your enthusiasm for Christ will be copied by others. Do not cause others to stumble—ever.

Be concerned for the needs of the church family. Be full of the Spirit and of wisdom. Be versed in the Scriptures and ready to witness for your Savior. Give careful attention to the office entrusted to you. Fulfill all its functions as unto the Lord. By accepting this trust, you indicate without reservation your commitment and loyalty to the message, doctrine, constitution, leadership and worldwide program of your church.

### Charge to officers

**Pastor:** Having prayerfully considered the nature and purpose of the work for which you have been chosen, will you consider your appointment a call from God? Are you willing to accept the duties of your office as responsibilities committed to you by the Lord of the Church? Will you seek to fulfill your responsibilities in the power of the Holy Spirit, and as unto the Lord Jesus Christ? If you will accept this charge, please respond by saying, "I do."

**Response by Officers:** I do.

### Charge to the congregation

**Pastor:** Since apostolic times, leadership of Christian churches has been entrusted to godly individuals. The Apostle Paul advised that they who ruled well should be counted worthy of double honor. A congregation which calls from among its members those to whom it gives special ministries must be supportive of the people whom it has chosen.

Do you, the members of this church, acknowledge and receive these leaders, entering with them into the spirit of the vows they have just made to God and this church? Do you promise to honor them, encourage them, cooperate with them and pray for them as the Word of God admonishes? If so, please affirm your acceptance of their spiritual oversight and support for them by rising to your feet.

**Response by Congregation:** (*The congregation will stand.*)

**Prayer of Installation** (The pastor prays, dedicating the leadership of the church to their tasks and to God and dedicating the congregation to renewed spiritual unity and progress under Jesus Christ, the Head of the Church.)

### INSTALLATION OF SUNDAY SCHOOL STAFF

The educational ministry of the church is unquestionably important. In an effort to engage only those individuals of the highest Christian character and commitment in this ministry, the church leadership should obtain promises of adherence to a "worker's covenant" on pages 142-144 and a signed questionnaire regarding child abuse (obtain from denominational office).

Those who fulfill this dimension of our Lord's commission to "make disciples" and to teach them to obey the Master's instructions should be properly recognized by the congregation and publicly consecrated to God. It is preferable to schedule the installation of Sunday school staff during the morning worship service of the first Sunday of the new Sunday school year.

### Outline for Installation of Sunday School Staff

**Hymn:** "A Charge to Keep I Have," "I Love to Tell the Story" or a chorus like "Shine, Jesus, Shine."

**Scripture reading:** Ephesians 4:11-16

**Charge to Sunday school staff**

**Pastor:** The Lord who called the Twelve, who commissioned and sent forth the seventy, who empowered the 120 in the upper room and who by the Holy Spirit selected the leaders of the apostolic Church, continues to call men and women into His service today. One of the wonderful calls upon men and women is the call to service through the educational ministries of the church. Your appointment to a teaching ministry needs to be perceived by you as a call from the Lord Jesus Himself! It is the call of the great Teacher who said, "Ye have not chosen me, but I have chosen you, and ordained you, that ye should go and bring forth fruit, and that your fruit should remain" (John 15:16).

Will you accept this call to service in our church as the call of God, committing yourselves without reservation to our church's message, teaching, leadership program and worldwide ministry? In dependence on God, do you pledge yourselves to teach the Bible, to faithfully fulfill all your duties, to live a consistent Christian life and to earnestly seek to win to Christ those under your care? If so, will you respond by saying, "We will"?

**Sunday school staff:** We will.

**Prayer of Installation** (*The minister will offer a prayer of thanksgiving to the Lord for those who have accepted His call to service in the Sunday school, dedicating the Sunday school staff to the Lord and asking for the Holy Spirit's empowerment and blessing on them and their work.*)

**Hymn:** Congregation sings one stanza of "Have Thine Own Way, Lord."

**Pastor:** To every member of the church family, may it in truth be said of us as we study together in the Sunday school this coming year, "Thy words were found, and I did eat them; and thy word was unto me the joy and rejoicing of mine heart" (Jeremiah 15:16).

Realizing that our Lord may return soon, and knowing the fields already are ripe for harvest, will you join the staff with your own consecration? "I beseech you therefore, brethren, by the mercies of God, that ye present your bodies a living sacrifice, holy, acceptable unto God, which is your reasonable service" (Romans 12:1). "Neither will I offer burnt offerings unto the LORD my God of that which doth cost me nothing" (2 Samuel 24:24).

**Pastor:** *(He invites the congregation to stand while he prays a prayer of consecration for both the staff and the people.)* Let us pray.

**Hymn:** "Fill Me Now"
**Benediction**

**Pastor:** "Now unto him that is able to do exceeding abundantly above all that we ask or think, according to the power that worketh in us, unto him be glory in the church by Christ Jesus throughout all ages, world without end. Amen" (Ephesians 3:20-21).

## WORKER'S COVENANT

Recognizing the high privilege that is mine to serve my Lord through our Sunday school and trusting in the help and guidance of the Holy Spirit, I earnestly pledge myself to this covenant.

1. I will at all times manifest a deep spiritual concern for the members of my class. My first desire shall be to bring about the salvation of each pupil who does not know the Lord Jesus and to encourage the spiritual growth of every Christian (Daniel 12:3).

2. I will carefully prepare my lessons and make each class session a matter of earnest prayer (1 Thessalonians 5:17).

3. I will be faithful in attendance and make it a practice to be present at least ten minutes early to welcome each pupil as he arrives. If at any time, through sickness or other emergency, I am unable to teach my class, I will notify my superintendent at the earliest possible moment (1 Corinthians 4:2).

4. I will teach according to the doctrines of our church, including Christ our Savior, Sanctifier, Healer and Coming King (Acts 20:27).

5. I will live what I teach in separation from the world and purity of life, "abstain[ing] from all appearance of evil" (1 Thessalonians 5:22) setting an example in dress, conversation, deportment and prayer (Ephesians 4:1).

6. I will regularly attend and urge members of my class to be present at the church services, recognizing that the church and Sunday school are inseparable. Believing in the importance of prayer, I will endeavor to maintain a regular attendance at the midweek prayer service, as well as Sunday services (Hebrews 10:24-25).

7. I will cooperate with the absentee program of our school and will strive to visit the home of each pupil at least once a year (Matthew 18:12).

8. I will wholeheartedly support the Sunday school program, endeavoring regularly to attend the monthly workers' conferences and the training classes (2 Timothy 2:15).

9. I understand that my appointment as a teacher is for the twelve-month period of the Sunday school year. Whether my appointment is made at the beginning or later in the year, I understand that it automatically terminates at the end of the Sunday school year (1 Corinthians 3:9).

10. I will cheerfully abide by the decisions of my church and Sunday school. I will cooperate with my fellow laborers in this teaching agency of our church so that our ministry will be effective and fruitful (Matthew 28:19-20; John 15:16).

_____ (signature)

_____ (date)

# 9 • Church Membership

CHURCH MEMBERSHIP may be stressed until quality is sacrificed and numbers become the only consideration. Or it may be neglected until the united strength of the church is lost in the informal relationship of those who gather week after week. Clearly, there is a desirable middle ground.

If spiritual standards of eligibility are to be maintained, a basic procedure is necessary. Even where there are denominational guidelines, the following fundamentals usually apply.

**1. Have an established standard of eligibility.** The minimum requirement would be satisfactory evidence of regeneration, conformity to the church's beliefs and acceptance of its constitution and bylaws.

**2. Have a properly authorized body whose responsibility it is to ascertain eligibility of applicants.** The church's board of elders, charged with the spiritual well-being of the membership, is the logical group.

**3. Require all applicants to be interviewed by this membership committee to determine their eligibility for membership.** Such an interview should be pleasant and informal without sacrificing its purpose. Should denominational policy or practice conflict with these provisions, the wise pastor will nevertheless fulfill their fundamental aim in a personal interview of each applicant.

## THE RECEPTION OF MEMBERS

Members may be received on communion Sunday or
during a regular worship service, the proper time within
the service being at the pastor's discretion. The pastor,
announcing the reception of members, will read the
names of those being received and the manner of their
reception—letter of transfer, confession of faith, re-
statement of faith.

The elders or the properly designated church officials
will take their place with the pastor in the front of the
sanctuary. Ushers, previously appointed to the task,
may escort those being received into membership to a
position in front of and facing the pastor and elders.
The ushers will then be seated. If parents or friends
who may have been responsible for the applicants coming to the church are present, invite them to stand with
the applicant during the ceremony.

**Pastor:** *(selecting from the following Scriptures)*

What shall I render unto the LORD
for all his benefits toward me? I will
take the cup of salvation, and call upon
the name of the LORD. I will pay my
vows unto the LORD now in the presence of all his people.

(Psalm 116:12-14)

For with the heart man believeth
unto righteousness; and with the

mouth confession is made unto salvation.

(Romans 10:10)

Whosoever therefore shall confess me before men, him will I confess also before my Father which is in heaven.

(Matthew 10:32)

And the Lord added to the church daily such as should be saved.

(Acts 2:47)

Blessed be the God and Father of our Lord Jesus Christ, which according to his abundant mercy hath begotten us again unto a lively hope by the resurrection of Jesus Christ from the dead, to an inheritance incorruptible, and undefiled, and that fadeth not away, reserved in heaven for you, who are kept by the power of God through faith unto salvation ready to be revealed in the last time.

(1 Peter 1:3-5)

### Covenant

**Pastor:** (*will read the following covenant*)

We, the members of this church, do solemnly covenant together with God, and with one another, that we will speak truthfully to one another, saying that which is "good to the use of edifying" (Ephesians 4:29). We shall "abstain from fleshly lusts, which war against the soul" (1 Peter 2:11); we will be kind to one another, putting away "all bitterness, and wrath, and anger, and clamour, and evil speaking" (Ephesians 4:31). We will be "kind one to another, tenderhearted, forgiving one another, even as God for Christ's sake hath forgiven [us]" (4:32).

We who are heads of families will observe the worship of God in our homes and will endeavor to lead our children, or others committed to our care, to a saving knowledge and personal faith in the Lord Jesus Christ. We will attend regularly, as far as Providence permits, the services of worship on the Lord's Day and such other services as the church may appoint.

We will observe together the Lord's Supper. We will aid, as the Lord prospers us, in the support of a faithful Christian ministry among us, and in sending the saving gospel of Christ to the whole human family.

We will remember those who are over us in the Lord, holding them in highest regard in love because of their work. For them we will faithfully pray, and with them we will faithfully labor as it may be our privilege.

God being our Helper, this we covenant to do.

### *Alternate Covenant*

**Minister:** As minister of this church it is my duty to inquire of you regarding your purpose of mind and heart. Do you believe in God as your Heavenly Father?

**Response:** I do.

**Minister:** Have you accepted Jesus Christ as your Savior and Lord?

**Response:** I have.

**Minister:** Will you strive to know and do the will of God as taught in Scripture?

**Response:** I will.

**Minister:** Will you be loyal to the church wherever you are, and uphold it by your prayers, your presence, your gifts and your service?

**Response:** I will.

**Minister:** (*to the candidates*) Christian friends, we rejoice in this expression of your desire to unite yourselves with us in this relationship. Because you have witnessed a good confession of faith, you are already one with the redeemed people of God of all generations. By uniting with this church, you enjoy all its sacred privileges and bear its responsibilities. It is your sacred obligation to uphold its testimony before everyone needing its message; to pray for its success; to give for its support; to attend its services and thus strengthen its ministry; in love, labor and sacrifice, to prosper its work, encourage its leaders and bring daily growth and enrichment to your own souls. Always walk worthy of the name of Christ and His church, avoiding every kind of evil. Love as brothers and sisters, and hold those who are over you in the Lord in highest regard in love because of their work.

**Minister:** (*to the congregation*) (*It would be appropriate to have them stand.*) Beloved, in receiving these Christian brothers [and/or sisters] into our fellowship we do enter into solemn covenant and obligation. Let them never find occasion to be ashamed of any of us or disappointed by our lives or testimony. May they ever find this house of God a place of spiritual enrichment, encouragement and refuge. We should always be ready to receive them as brothers and sisters, bear their burdens in the love of Christ and share with them the deepest needs of life. All that the Word of God has led them to expect to find among the redeemed should be found here. We shall, by the grace of God, in receiving them into our fellowship, pledge to them in like manner as we have required them to pledge all that is consistent with a godly life. May our communion be sweet and our joy full.

The pastor will pray a brief prayer of dedication at this point. Then he will shake hands with each new member, personally welcoming each one into membership. He will also at this time present each one with a membership certificate or a Bible or some other suitable token of commemoration. It would also be appropriate to give each new member a box of offering envelopes as an encouragement to his spiritual expression and worship of the God who supplies all his needs.

**Hymn:** "Blest Be the Tie That Binds" or "Bind Us Together" may be sung at the conclusion (if desired).

**Benediction** (A benediction of blessing like the following would be appropriate at the end of the ceremony.)

**Minister:** As you share in this great hour of worship, and move toward the days, weeks and months to come, may the God who creates bless you. May the God who redeems bring you joy. May the God who sustains empower you to share the abundant life in all that you do. May the God who patiently waits for you give you love and care forever. In Christ's name. Amen.

If ushers have been used, they may now escort the new members to their seats.

**Note:** The minister will see that the official membership records of the church are properly inscribed with the members' names (correctly spelled) and the date of the occasion.

### *MEMBERSHIP LETTERS*

**Request for transfer:** If the applicant for membership is known to have membership in another church, the courteous thing to do is to suggest that it be transferred. Because most members profess ignorance as to how to transfer a membership, the minister will suggest that he be permitted to write for the letter of transfer. Here is a sample letter:

Dear Christian friends:

At the request of [applicant's name], I am writing to ask for the transfer of his/her letter of membership to this church. He/she has signified his/her desire to be received into our fellowship at the next reception of members, which is to be soon [or specify actual date].

Your early reply will be sincerely appreciated.

Cordially yours,

[name and signature]

If the applicant expresses the desire to obtain the letter of transfer himself or herself, this is acceptable. Here is a sample letter:

Dear Christian friends:

Since I am no longer part of your fellowship, and since I have found a new church home, I respectfully request that a letter of membership transfer be issued on my behalf and mailed to: [name and address of new church].

I understand that when this letter is issued and received, my membership in your fellowship will cease.

Thank you for your prompt attention to this matter.

I also thank you for your past input in my life and wish you God's continued blessing.

Sincerely,

[name and signature]

**Note:** Some denominations may require that letters requesting or issuing transfer of membership be signed by the church secretary or some similar official, but the minister may still use his position to expedite such matters.

**Issuance of transfer:** Again, a simple letter on church stationery will suffice:

Dear Christian friends:

This is to certify that [applicant's name] is a member in good and regular standing and in full fellowship with this church. As such, we commend him/her to your Christian love and oversight.

Membership in this church ceases with the issuance of this letter. [*Or*, Membership in this church is continued until notified of his reception elsewhere. *Or*, When he/she shall have so united, his/her connection with us will cease.]

Cordially yours,

[name & signature]

# 10 • Dedication of a Baby or Child

ALTHOUGH SOME CHURCHES baptize infants, most evangelicals feel that Christ intended baptism to be for those who have come into the Christian faith through repentance and the new birth. It is a voluntary rite, testifying to a spiritual transaction within. As such, it should be reserved for those who have reached an age of understanding.

In place of infant baptism, the practice of dedicating children to God has become widely observed. Not surprisingly, there is wide latitude in the interpretation of the rite. If parents in the early Church formally dedicated their children to God, there is no biblical mention of such a ceremony, but there are such precedents as Hannah's dedication of Samuel and Joseph and Mary's presentation of Jesus.

The dedication act is recognition of the Lordship of Jesus Christ. Parents who have offered themselves "a living sacrifice" desire to publicly extend that offering to their most priceless possessions—their children. The more we attach spiritual significance to the rite, the more inclined we must be to reserve this ceremony for parents who themselves are committed wholly to Christ and His purposes.

The minister, upon learning of the parents' desire to dedicate their child, will visit them in their home to discuss with them the service and its significance. The door is usually wide open at this time for his approach to their personal spiritual needs. If they were prompted by sentiment rather than devotion, he can tactfully show them the difference and draw them to the spiritual purpose. Should they be unbelievers, the minister has an unparalleled opportunity to invite them to come to God themselves prior to bringing their child.

Single-parent families are more and more a reality in our changing society. If the parent offering his or her child has sole responsibility for the child's upbringing, there would seem to be no reason not to solemnize the parent's desire to dedicate his or her child to the Lord. If the absent parent maintains some custodial right to the child and he or she is not in sympathy with the covenant of dedication, the minister will need to exercise careful discretion before consenting to dedicate the child.

The minister will explain the manner of the service and when it will be scheduled in the worship service. (It is wise to put it early in the worship hour, before the child becomes restless.) He will also obtain the correctly spelled name of the child and the child's date of birth. This information will later be entered in the church records and on a certificate that the minister will give the parents following the service.

## THE SERVICE OF DEDICATION

**Musical Interlude or Hymn:** (The organist may play softly or the congregation may sing an appropriate hymn such as "Jewels" or "Jesus Loves Me," while an appointed usher may bring the parents forward with their child to stand before the minister. The father will hold the child in his arms if an infant.)

**Minister:** (*The minister may read one or more of the following Scriptures.*)

Hear, O Israel; the LORD our God is one LORD: And thou shalt love the LORD thy God with all thine heart, and with all thy soul, and with all thy might. And these words, which I command thee this day, shall be in thine heart: And thou shalt teach them diligently unto thy children, and shalt talk of them when thou sittest in thine house, and when thou walkest by the way, and when thou liest down, and when thou risest up.

(Deuteronomy 6:4-7)

But the mercy of the LORD is from everlasting to everlasting upon them that fear him, and his righteousness unto children's children; to such as keep his covenant, and to those that remember his commandments to do them.

(Psalm 103:17-18)

And they brought young children to him, that he should touch them: and his disciples rebuked those that brought them. But when Jesus saw it, he was much displeased, and said unto them, Suffer the little children to come unto me, and forbid them not: for of such is the kingdom of God. Verily I say unto you, Whosoever shall not receive the kingdom of God as a little child, he shall not enter therein. And he took them up in his arms, put his hands upon them, and blessed them.

(Mark 10:13-16)

And Jesus called a little child unto him, and set him in the midst of them, and said, Verily I say unto you, Except ye be converted, and become as little children, ye shall not enter the kingdom of heaven. Whosoever therefore shall humble himself as this little child, the same is greatest in the kingdom of heaven. And whoso shall receive one such little child in my name receiveth me. But whoso shall offend one of these little ones which believe in me, it were better for him that a millstone were hanged about his neck, and that he were drowned in the depth of the sea.

(Matthew 18:2-6)

**Minister:** (*Speaking to the parents*) Throughout the ages, godly parents have presented their children to the Lord in dedication. You follow a noble heritage. In presenting your child to the Lord, you enter into a solemn relationship with God, who keeps His covenant to a thousand generations.

While dedication is a worthy act, you must understand that it offers no saving virtue. Dedication does not guarantee your child's salvation, for this requires a personal commitment that each one must make on his own upon reaching the age of awareness and accountability. Salvation is obtained by grace, through faith in Jesus Christ as personal Savior and upon repentance. Though the dedication ceremony does not save, it is nonetheless a most significant act of faith and declaration of intent by the parents to provide Christian nurture to their child.

Believing that this child is a gift from God, and that He shall hold you accountable for him [her], do you now solemnly confess that it is your purpose to dedicate this child to the Lord and to His service? Will you pray with him [her] and for him [her]; instruct him [her] faithfully in the doctrines of the Christian faith; teach him [her] to read the Word of God; to pray and to lead a holy life; take him [her] faithfully to the house of worship to attend its services; and do all that is in your power to bring him [her] to the knowledge of Jesus Christ as Savior and Lord?

**Parents:** We will.

**Minister:** (*The minister takes the child in his arms or places his hand on the child's head and prays.*) _____ [child's name], I dedicate you to God in the name of the Father and of the Son and of the Holy Spirit, and I loose you from the powers of darkness. May your young life be nurtured and matured under the gracious influence of the Holy Spirit. May God protect you physically and deliver you from temptation. May He early call you into His kingdom and ultimately into His service, using you to advance His glory and to hasten the coming of our Lord Jesus Christ. Amen.

(*The minister, if he is holding the infant, will return him or her to the parents, at the same time giving to the parent who does not have the child the previously prepared certificate of dedication. The usher will then escort the parents back to their seats.*)

## An Alternate Service of Dedication

**Note:** This service calls for a rosebud, a red carnation and a white carnation to be displayed on a table at the front of the sanctuary.

**Parental dedication**

**Minister:** _____[name of parents] bring their son [daughter], _____ [name of child], to publicly dedicate themselves and this son [daughter] to the Lord Jesus Christ.

**Scripture**

**Minister:** Hear the Word of God:

Hear, O Israel: the LORD our God is one LORD: And thou shalt love the LORD thy God with all thine heart, and with all thy soul, and with all thy might. And these words, which I command thee this day, shall be in thine heart: And thou shalt teach them diligently unto thy children, and shalt talk of them when thou sittest in thine house, and when thou walkest by the way, and when thou liest down, and when thou risest up. And thou shalt bind them for a sign upon thine hand, and they shall be as frontlets between thine eyes. And thou shalt write them upon the posts of thy house, and on thy gates.

(Deuteronomy 6:4-9)

At the same time came the disciples unto Jesus, saying, Who is the greatest in the kingdom of heaven? And Jesus called a little child unto him, and set him in the midst of them, and said, Verily I say unto you, Except ye be converted, and become as little children, ye shall not enter into the kingdom of heaven. Whosoever therefore shall humble himself as this little child, the same is greatest in the kingdom of heaven. And whoso shall receive one such little child in my name receiveth me. But whoso shall offend one of these little ones which believe in me, it were better for him that a millstone were hanged about his neck, and that he were drowned in the depth of the sea.

(Matthew 18:1-6)

**Charge to the parents**

**Minister:** In presenting yourselves and your child to the Lord, you enter into a solemn relationship with our God who keeps His covenants to a thousand generations. This is a serious vow for which God will hold you personally responsible.

I charge you in the presence of God and this congregation to love your child as much as your own life. Never allow him [her] to ever have any doubts of the depths of your love.

Teach him [her] to love and obey God. Let him see in your life evidences of the working of your personal Savior. Make spiritual things the topic of conversation, the focus of family life and the basis for personal development.

Teach him [her] to love and obey you. Obedience of parents is right. When _____ [name of baby] honors you, God promises him [her] long life.

The nurturing of _____ [name of baby] is your combined responsibility—yours and yours alone. Be concerned about every facet of his [her] life.

On the table is a bouquet of three flowers. The rosebud represents _____ [name of baby]. He [she] is just beginning to develop. May he [she], because of your faithfulness, gloriously flower for the glory of God.

### Charge to the father

**Minister:** _____ [father's name], you are the father. The Bible has specific directions for you.

> Husbands, love your wives, even as Christ also loved the church, and gave himself for it. . . . He that loveth his wife loveth himself. . . . And, ye fathers, provoke not your children to wrath: but bring them up in the nurture and admonition of the Lord.
>
> (Ephesians 5:25, 28, 6:4)

The red carnation symbolizes you, the father. It stands for strength and courage. God expects you to be strong. Your wife and your son [daughter] should never doubt that you love them. There must be a willingness on your part to place their welfare far ahead of your own. Your manner of life should draw your son [daughter] like a magnet to the Lord Jesus Christ.

### Charge to the mother

**Minister:** _____ [mother's name], you are the mother. The white carnation speaks of your purity. God has commanded that you be submissive to and respectful of your husband. This is to be a willing exercise on your part. You are to maintain an open, gentle and loving relationship with him and your child. Your love, concern and teaching will be a major factor in your son [daughter] coming to an early knowledge of the Savior.

**Vow of the parents**

**Minister:** Believing that _____ [name of baby] is a gift from God and that God will hold you accountable for him [her], do you now solemnly confess that it is your purpose to dedicate him [her] to the Lord and to His service? Will you faithfully discharge your God-given responsibilities as parents, as outlined in God's Word? Will you pray with and for him [her]; instruct him [her] faithfully in the teachings of God's Holy Word; teach him [her] to read the Word of God, to pray and to lead a holy life; take him [her] faithfully to a place of worship; and do all that in you lies to bring him [her] to the knowledge of Jesus Christ as Savior and Lord? If you will, answer, "I will."

**Parents:** I will.

**Vows of the congregation**

**Minister:** (*Parents and child turn to face the congregation*) As a local congregation we bear a responsibility to this family. Will you pray for this family, encourage them as they grow together and do all that is in your power to assist in _____ [name of child] coming to know Jesus Christ as personal Savior and Lord? If you will make that covenant with this family, please stand.

**Response by Congregation** (*The congregation will stand.*)

**Prayer of Dedication** (*Parents turn and face the pastor as he prays first for them and then for the child.*)

# 11 • Consecration Services for Christian Workers

Blessed is the church that has many of its sons and daughters called into active Christian service. The local congregation will not only want to recognize, but also to "set apart" those who leave it for such service. The ties between congregation and worker are the richer and the stronger when this is done.

A service of consecration is not to duplicate or be a substitute for the more formal procedure of ordination. Rather, it is performed to give spiritual recognition to the worker and his or her task, and to further the church's interest in his or her life and ministry. Such a service should be brief and devoid of ostentation. It will be most effective when planned as a part of the regular order of worship.

## THE CONSECRATION SERVICE

At the designated place in the order of service, the minister will announce the consecration service. The one or ones being set apart will be brought to the front by an usher, if they are not already seated there. Officers or representatives of every department of the church should also be near the front.

**Scripture:** The minister will read one or more of the following Scriptures:

And Moses said unto the LORD, See, thou sayest unto me, Bring up this people: and thou hast not let me know whom thou wilt send with me. Yet thou hast said, I know thee by name, and thou hast also found grace in my sight. Now therefore, I pray thee, if I have found grace in thy sight, shew me now thy way, that I may know thee, that I may find grace in thy sight: and consider that this nation is thy people. And he said, My presence shall go with thee, and I will give thee rest. And he said unto him, If thy presence go not with me, carry us not up hence. For wherein shall it be known here that I and thy people have found grace in thy sight? is it not in that thou goest with us? so shall we be separated, I and thy people, from all the people that are upon the face of the earth. And the LORD said unto Moses, I will do this thing also that thou hast spoken: for thou hast found grace in my sight, and I know thee by name.

(Exodus 33:12-17)

And when the seventh month came, the children of Israel were in their cities. And all the people gathered themselves together as one man into the street that was before the water gate; and they spake unto Ezra the scribe to bring the book of the law of Moses, which the LORD had commanded to Israel. And Ezra the priest brought the law before the congregation both of men and women, and all that could hear with understanding, upon the first day of the seventh month. And he read therein before the street that was before the water gate from the morning until midday, before the men and the women, and those that could understand; and the ears of all the people were attentive unto the book of the law. . . . And Ezra opened the book in the sight of all the people; (for he was above all the people;) and when he opened it, all the people stood up: And Ezra blessed the LORD, the great God. And all the people answered, Amen, Amen, with lifting up their hands: and they bowed their heads, and worshipped the LORD with their faces to the ground. . . . So they read in the book in the law of God distinctly, and gave the sense, and caused them to understand the reading.

(Nehemiah 7:73-8:3, 5-6, 8)

As they ministered to the Lord, and fasted, the Holy Ghost said, Separate me Barnabas and Saul for the work whereunto I have called them. And when they had fasted and prayed, and laid their hands on them, they sent them away.

(Acts 13:2-3)

**Minister:** (*Addressing the one [ones] being set apart*) _____ [name(s) of worker(s)], will you now stand before this congregation and declare to them the call of God upon your life and the purpose for which you go forth to serve?

**Christian worker:** (*This gives the Christian worker an opportunity to testify briefly and to appeal for the interest and prayer support of the home church.*)

**Minister:** (*Addressing entire congregation*) Who of this congregation, thankful that God has called _____ and _____ [name(s) of workers] into active Christian service, will extend to him [them] their encouragement in this under-taking, their promise of loving support, their assurance of faithful prayer? Let all who are willing stand to their feet. (*Pause for people to stand.*)

**Minister:** (*Addressing the one(s) being set apart*) _____ [person's name], please kneel here, while the officers of this church join me in laying hands upon you and praying the prayer of consecration.

**Prayer:** *The minister prays. At the conclusion, the church officers will take time to extend their personal benediction to the one(s) set apart.*

**Presentation:** *(optional) If so desired, the minister may present to the person(s) being consecrated some token of the church's esteem and continuing interest.*

**Hymn:** "Blest Be the Tie That Binds" or some other suitable song or chorus.

## AN ALTERNATE COMMISSIONING AFFIRMATION

**Minister:**_____ [name of worker(s)], you are Christ's ambassador(s) and our representative(s) to _____ [*identify country or people group*]. Today, as a body of believers with a heart for a lost world, we send you. With full hearts, we send you. With gratitude for your part in fulfilling the Great Commission of Jesus Christ, we send you. As the Father sent Jesus, so Jesus sends you and so we send you. As the New Testament Church sent their trained members into every corner of the known world, so we send you to _____ [*name the country or people group*]. We are the Church of Jesus Christ and we send you.

**Responsive Reading:** (*The following text could be placed in the bulletin and then read responsively by the pastor and the congregation.*)

We send you to the harassed and helpless, like sheep without a shepherd—
*Have compassion for them like Jesus had.*
To those without hope and without God—
*Be the aroma of Christ through your presence with them.*
To those who have been darkened in their understanding—
*Bring the light of the knowledge of the glory of God.*
To those who are perishing—
*Speak life.*
To those who are lost—
*Bring home.*
With the poor in body and spirit—
*Share your gifts and the riches of Christ.*
To the sick of heart and body and mind—

*Be a vessel of the Great Physician.*

Bind up the broken, lift up the fallen, preach Good News to the poor and proclaim the year of the Lord's favor. Because we send you in Christ's place, do as He did.

Whether it is the skill of dentistry, a cup of cold water, a friendly chat or a warm smile that you share, we are sending you to do it in His Name. Go with our blessing and His anointing, our prayers and His enabling, our provisions and His empowering. We commission you [*include the family here*] to go in Jesus' name. And all of God's people said, "Amen!"

# 12 • Ceremonies for Buildings

## A GROUNDBREAKING CEREMONY

INASMUCH AS THIS IS AN OUTDOOR SERVICE, it should be held on a day with appropriate weather conditions. The time of the service must also be adjusted to the convenience of the congregation. If the place where the ceremony is to be held is near the house of worship, it is generally best to plan the service in conjunction with a regular gathering of the congregation. The order of service should be reproduced and distributed to all present so they can participate. Encourage the people to move in close so everyone can hear the ceremony.

### The Ceremony

**Prayer:** The minister should open in prayer, invoking God's presence. If so desired, the prayer can conclude with the Lord's Prayer recited in unison.

**Responsive reading**

**Hymn or special music:** This will be limited to very familiar music if an instrument or instruments are not available.

**Brief remarks:** The minister or guest official will speak of the building to be erected and the aim for its use as a house of worship, an educational unit or parsonage.

**Groundbreaking:** The minister or some specially selected or honored person will take the shovel and remove the first spade of earth. Other officers and leaders may be designated to follow, each removing a shovelful of earth.

**Prayer:** The minister should pray for the furtherance of this undertaking, that it might be to the glory of God and the common good.

**Hymn or special music**
**Benediction**

## LAYING A CORNERSTONE

The laying of the cornerstone is a joyous moment in the life of a congregation. By proper care and planning, it can have great spiritual significance, too.

The contents of the weather-sealed box that is to be placed in the cornerstone will of course be determined and prepared beforehand. Customarily such a box contains a Bible, a written history of the church, an accurate membership roll, a list of officers, the names of the building committee and possibly even an honor roll of contributors who are making the building possible.

It is important to consult the contractor for instructions about putting on the mortar and setting the stone. If the contractor can be present for the service, so much the better.

All who have part in the ceremony will be instructed as to what they are to do. Copies of the service order and a listing of the contents of the box should be reproduced for all in attendance.

### The Cornerstone Ceremony

**Doxology**
**Invocation and Lord's Prayer**
**Hymn:** A suitable hymn, such as "The Church's One Foundation," or "Cornerstone" may be used.

**Scripture:** First Corinthians 3:10-17 or First Peter 2:4-10 are both appropriate.

**Prayer:** This could be offered by a guest official, the chairman of the building committee or a leading elder.

**Special music**

**Brief remarks:** These could be by the minister or a guest chosen for the occasion.

**Laying of the cornerstone:** This should be performed by the minister with assistance from the chairman of the building committee and possibly one other designated person.

**Prayer of thanksgiving:** This prayer should include thanks for progress on the building, for safety for those who are working on its construction, for the expectations as the building is completed and occupied.

**Concluding hymn:** Use the hymn "Great Is Thy Faithfulness."

**Benediction**

## DEDICATION OF A CHURCH BUILDING

No other hour in a church's history quite compares with the dedication of a new building. Nor is any other service looked forward to with such enthusiastic anticipation. Such a service, to be worthy of all the factors that have brought it about, must seek to capture the spirit of exultation that is naturally present and direct it to the highest spiritual plane. The burning vision, the tireless labors, the spirit of sacrifice, the thankfulness to God, the love and loyalty to Christ and His Church are all elements to be considered.

Let good taste and sensible length be the guide when planning a dedicatory service. Some congregations want all their former pastors to be present and participate. Others want all the Christian organizations of the community to be represented. Still others will think every department of the church should be included.

Taking all this into account, it is easy to see how the program can become complex as well as lengthy. The minister should show consideration for all concerned and attempt to arrive at a happy and acceptable consensus. Choosing who will be included in the program is as important as properly instructing each person involved about his or her part and, in the case of those who are speaking, what the time limitations are.

The entire service, including the responses in the act of dedication and possibly even the words of the hymns being used, should be printed and available to all.

## *The Dedication Service*

**Prelude**
**Hymn:** Use "All Hail the Power of Jesus' Name" and have the congregation stand.
**The Call to Worship**

**Minister:** Who shall ascend into the hill of the LORD? or who shall stand in his holy place?

**Congregation:** He that hath clean hands, and a pure heart; who hath not lifted up his soul unto vanity, nor sworn deceitfully.

**Minister:** He shall receive the blessing from the LORD, and righteousness from the God of his salvation. This is the generation of them that seek him, that seek thy face, O Jacob.

**Congregation:** Lift up your heads, O ye gates; and be ye lift up, ye everlasting doors; and the King of glory shall come in.

**Minister:** Who is this King of glory?

**Congregation:** The LORD strong and mighty—he is the King of glory.

(Psalm 24:3-8, 10)

**Invocation and the Lord's Prayer**

**Scripture:** Use either Second Chronicles 5:13-6:2, 40-42 or Psalm 84 or First Peter 2:4-10.

**Special music:** An appropriate selection would be "Bless This House."

**Recognitions and acknowledgments**

**Presentation of keys:** Either the chairman of the building committee or the contractor will speak of the financial and time investment represented by the building and cite pertinent facts concerning its construction. As this person concludes, he will present the keys to the minister or the chairman of the board of trustees who will respond appropriately. (Some states do not require a board of trustees. If this is the case in your state, the board having custodial responsibility for the church property should be substituted.)

*or*

**Minister:** (*calling board of trustees to platform and addressing them*) You have been selected by the members of this church as trustees of this house of worship now being dedicated to the service of Almighty God. Protect it at all times; preserve it for continued service; improve it as need and opportunity arise. To you is committed the task of keeping it worthy of its name—a house of worship.

From this time forth, you will hold this property in trust for God and this church. May Christian faith, hope and love dwell in your hearts, and may the Holy Spirit guide and direct you in all the activities that fall within the sphere of your responsibility as trustees.

**Trustees:** (*responding in unison*) We, the Board of Trustees of this church, do covenant with God and one another to discharge our duties faithfully. May this house of worship at all times magnify the preaching of the Word of God and fulfill in this community and worldwide all the purposes for which it is now being set apart.

**The act of dedication**

**Minister:** To the glory of God the Father, to the honor of the Lord Jesus Christ, His Son and our Savior, and to the praise of the Holy Spirit, our Comforter, . . .

**Congregation:** . . . we dedicate this house.

**Minister:** For worship in prayer and praise, for the ministry of the Word of God, for the celebration of the church's ordinances, for the guidance of children and the sanctification of the family, . . .

**Congregation:** . . . we dedicate this house.

**Minister:** For the teaching of the Word of God, for the seeking of the salvation of mankind, for the witnessing of Christ's saving gospel to the uttermost parts of the earth, in the hope of the soon appearing of our glorious Lord and coming King, . . .

**Minister and congregation:** (*together*) . . . to God the Father, God the Son and God the Holy Spirit—eternal, holy and glorious Trinity, three Persons, one God—to You we dedicate this church.

**Prayer of dedication:** This prayer may be offered by a denominational official, if one is present, or by the minister.

**Hymn:** Use one such as "The Church's One Foundation."

**Congratulations:** Brief remarks by former pastors.

**Special music**

**Dedicatory sermon**

**Offering**

**Closing hymn:** Use "Take My Life, and Let It Be."

**Benediction**

**Postlude**

### AN ALTERNATE ACT OF DEDICATION

**Minister:** Because we have purposed in our hearts to build a sanctuary to the worship of the true and living God, and to the service of Jesus Christ our Lord, I call upon this congregation to stand for the holy act of dedication. (*Congregation stands.*) To the glory of God the Father; to the honor of Jesus Christ the Son; to the praise of the Holy Spirit . . .

**Congregation:** . . . we dedicate this house.

**Minister:** Knowing there is no other name under heaven given to men by which we must be saved . . .

**Congregation:** . . . we dedicate this house to the bringing of the saving knowledge of our Lord Jesus Christ to the unconverted.

**Minister:** In obedience to the explicit command of Christ to go into all the world and preach the good news to all creation . . .

**Congregation:** . . . we dedicate this house to the worldwide task of the whole church of Christ, until the kingdom of this world has become the kingdom of our Lord and of His Christ.

**Minister:** Realizing the obligation to bring up our children in the training and instruction of the Lord . . .

**Congregation:** . . . we dedicate this house to the making sacred of the home and family life; to the religious nurture and education of children, youth and adults; to the grace of Christian character and the warmth of Christian fellowship.

**Minister:** In obedience to the command of Christ to love our neighbors as ourselves . . .

**Congregation:** . . . we dedicate this house to the fellowship of the saints, to the refuge of weary, restless people, to the peace and hope of the oppressed, to the comfort of those who mourn and to the happiness of all those who share our faith.

**Minister and congregation:** (*together*) We, the members and friends of this church, deeply grateful for the heritage that has been entrusted to us and keenly conscious of those ties by which we are bound to the Lord of all life and to each other, do covenant together in this act of dedication, offering ourselves anew to the work and worship of our Heavenly Father, through Jesus Christ our Lord. Amen.

### DEDICATION OF A CHILD CARE CENTER OR CHRISTIAN SCHOOL

**Director:** We have purposed in our hearts to establish a Child Care Center to the honor of the true and living God and as an extension of His Church into the community, reaching out to the people for whom we care. We will assist parents by providing a safe and healthy Christian atmosphere and quality early childhood education for their preschool children. We pledge ourselves to provide a rich and varied program of activities to promote the emotional, social, spiritual, physical and intellectual growth of the child and to strengthen parents and families through a Christ-centered program.

**Congregation:** We dedicate the _____ [name of center] Child Care Center.

**Director:** Knowing that there is none other name under heaven given among men whereby we must be saved—

**Congregation:** We dedicate this center to the bringing of the saving knowledge of our Lord Jesus Christ to the unconverted.

**Director:** Realizing the obligation to bring up our children in the nurture and admonition of the Lord—

**Congregation:** We dedicate this Center to the sanctity of the home and the hallowing of family life; to the religious nurture and education of children; to the grace of Christian character and the warmth of Christian fellowship.

**Director:** In obedience to the command of Christ to love our neighbors as ourselves—

**Congregation:** We dedicate the Child Care Center as an expression of our love for Christ and our love and concern for those outside the fold of His salvation.

**Director:** For the teaching of the Bible; for the seeking of the salvation of mankind; for the development of Christian character in children; and in service to our Christ and our community—

**Director and Congregation:** (*together*) We, the members and friends of _____ [name of church], deeply grateful for the heritage that has been entrusted to us, and keenly conscious of those ties by which we are bound to the Lord of all life and to each other, do covenant together in this act of dedication, offering ourselves anew to the work and worship of our Heavenly Father, through Jesus Christ our Lord. Amen.

**Prayer of dedication**

## DEDICATION OF A PARSONAGE OR CHRISTIAN HOME

The importance of the home in God's plan makes it altogether fitting for even the dwelling itself to be set apart to the Lord. Such devotion would have the beneficial effect of strengthening and preserving the sanctity of the Christian home. With this in mind, let the church set an example, if it buys or builds a parsonage, and let members of the congregation, when they buy or build, set their homes apart to God. Such a service can be of untold blessing to all concerned.

As with other ceremonies involving those present, it is important to have copies of the service order available for all in attendance.

**Note:** Prepare a loaf of bread and place it on a table, to be broken during this ceremony.

## The Ceremony of Dedication

**Hymn:** Use "All for Jesus" or "Take My Life and Let It Be" sung by the assembled group or selected singers.
**Invocation**
**Special music:** A soloist or group might sing "Bless This House" or, in the absence of singers, the minister may wish to read the words.

**Minister:** We are assembled to dedicate this dwelling to God as a Christian home. It is our hope and faith that it will be a place of happiness, adding to life's meaning for all who shall call it "home."

The home was the first institution God our Father established for His children. Before the church and before any form of civil government, the home was a divine institution. Love was the first bond which linked human lives together, and the home was its expression. The home became the nursery of true faith, of education, of culture, of beauty, of civilization. In all the course of history, the home is still the greatest of human institutions and the most vital expression of the presence of God.

The home is where we find protection from the elements, where food is prepared for nourishment and where beds are provided for rest from the wearying tasks of life. The home is also a symbol of the heavenly home that our Lord has gone to prepare for all His redeemed ones. We have "a building of God, an house not made with hands, eternal in the heavens" (2 Corinthians 5:1) prepared for us. In this service we now dedicate this home to the Christian ideals for which it was intended, to happiness and peace and to faith in God through our Lord Jesus Christ. "Except the LORD build the house, they labour in vain that build it" (Psalm 127:1).

**Minister:** (*The minister will take bread from the table and break it, giving one piece to the head of the home, another to an invited guest and retaining a third piece for himself.*) One of the most basic acts of hospitality is the sharing of bread. For people to break bread together—to be nourished by the same loaf—is a symbol of the life we share. The most familiar prayer among Christians is in the petition, "Give us today our daily bread." (*The three will eat their portions of bread. As they do so, the others present will prepare to participate in the dedication liturgy.*)

**Minister:** With thankfulness for the faithful artisans who have constructed this dwelling, giving it strength against the elements and beauty and utility for those who will live here, . . .

**Response:** . . . we dedicate this house.

**Minister:** With the prayer that it be protected from fire, storm, vandalism and all manner of calamity . . .

**Response:** . . . we dedicate this house.

**Minister:** With thanks to God for the beauty of light to shine through its windows and the beauty of nature and community to surround it, . . .

**Response:** . . . we dedicate this house.

**Minister:** With anticipation of the ministry this home may have to neighbors, friends, relatives, our church people and others who will knock at and enter these doors, . . .

**Response:** . . . we dedicate this house.

**Minister:** To all the sweetness and hallowed joys of home life, to all the hopes of future happiness through God's unmeasured gift of years, . . .

**Response:** . . . we dedicate this house.

**Minister:** To the glory of Jesus Christ, our Savior and Lord, and to His honor as Head of this home, . . .

**Response:** . . . we dedicate this house.

**Benediction:** (*pronounced by the minister*)

The LORD bless thee, and keep thee:
The LORD make his face shine upon
thee, and be gracious unto thee: The
LORD lift up his countenance upon
thee, and give thee peace.

(Numbers 6:24-26)

### BURNING A MORTGAGE

Involvement in debt is a common and usually un-
avoidable experience for a church. Even under the best
of circumstances, it is a burden from which the church
is happy to be released. The day the mortgage is burned
will rank among the outstanding events of the church's
history. It is a matter of local preference whether this
event should be observed at a special service or incorporated into the order of a regular service. A wide range of
people may be included in the ceremony: one or all of
the original note-signers, a representative or officer
from each department of the church, former pastors,
denominational officials.

Two things are important to remember. First, the
original mortgage document is valuable. It should be
carefully preserved among the church's papers. Only a
*copy* of the mortgage document should be used for the
burning ceremony. Second, the burning of the mortgage
is a fire hazard. Safety precautions should include a
metal pan large enough to contain the flames and ashes.
Be sure to insulate the pan from the stand or table on
which it rests. A suitable fire extinguisher should be
out of sight but ready in case of need.

The document may be divided into several strips,
each being held and ignited by those participating. Or

participants may each hold a lighted taper, together applying their flames to the document. Or one person, representing all, may burn the mortgage.

If the ceremony is to be celebrated as a special service, the following order of service may be expanded by additional music and extended remarks.

## The Mortgage-Burning Ceremony

**Hymn:** *(If not already on the platform, participants may assemble during the singing of a hymn of thanksgiving.)*

**Scripture:** Psalm 126 or 2 Corinthians 9:6-15 is appropriate.

**Prayer:** The minister could do this or ask a designated guest.

**Remarks:** Reminisce on the events in the church's history leading up to the present moment. The number of participants and the time allotted to each will necessarily be brief if this ceremony is part of a regular service. The minister will conclude with a summation and an invitation to the platform of participants involved in the mortgage burning.

**The burning of the mortgage**

**Doxology:** *(The congregation standing.)*

**Closing prayer**

## OTHER CEREMONIES

Occasionally a congregation will want to formally dedicate new church furnishings—a piano, an organ, flags, communionware. Usually such a dedication is scheduled within a regular service of the church. This would be true even if the object was a new organ and the dedication took place in conjunction with a specially called recital. From the above outlines and suggestions, it should be relatively easy to create a brief, but appropriate order of service for the dedication of such furnishings.

## LIFTING A DEDICATION

There comes the happy moment in the growth and development of many congregations when new and larger quarters must be built. In most cases this involves a move to a new location. Sometimes, the old property which must be disposed of is acquired by another religious body, a lodge or some commercial interest. Since the premises are to be no longer occupied by their former owners, nor used for their specific purposes, it is fitting that their act of dedication be revoked.

The lifting of the dedication will, therefore, include the removal of the cornerstone and its contents, the removal of the church's name and identifying insignia and everything sacred to its usage. Thus, in a spiritual sense at least, the memories and attachments of the old will be lifted and moved to the new place of abode.

The ceremony for the lifting of the dedication should follow the last service in the building, if possible. The cornerstone will have been loosened from its mortar so it can be easily and quickly removed during the ceremony. All participants in the service will have been carefully instructed by the minister as to what they are to do and when they are to do it. Though the service is quite brief, the entire order should be printed and distributed to all present so they can take part.

### The Ceremony

**Minister:**

And, Thou, Lord, in the beginning hast laid the foundation of the earth; and the heavens are the works of thine hands: They shall perish; but thou remainest; and they all shall wax old as doth a garment; and as a vesture shalt thou fold them up, and they shall be changed: but thou art the same, and thy years shall not fail.

(Hebrews 1:10-12)

**Congregation:** As the earth and the heavens shall be set aside when they in God's wisdom have served their purposes, so we would set aside this house as having served its useful purpose as our place of worship.

**Minister:** Concerning the law of devoted things we read:

And when a man shall sanctify his house to be holy unto the LORD, then the priest shall estimate it, whether it be good or bad: as the priest shall estimate it, so shall it stand. And if he that sanctified it will redeem his house, then he shall add the fifth part of the money of thy estimation unto it, and it shall be his.

(Leviticus 27:14-15)

**Congregation:** As Israel was allowed to redeem devoted things and the proceeds of the redemption price used to the good of the sanctuary, so the money realized in the sale of this building shall go toward the building of a more appropriate place of worship.

**Pastor:** Because that Thou, O Lord, has enabled this people in faith to move forward toward acquiring a more appropriate place of worship, we therefore lift the dedication of this building in the name of the Father, and of the Son and of the Holy Ghost.

**Trustees:** We, the Board of Trustees of this church, will no longer hold this property in trust for God and this congregation. (*Here the trustees remove the cornerstone.*)

This cornerstone, symbol of Christ, the true foundation and cornerstone of His Church, we have removed that it may serve as a token to all that this building will no longer be recognized as our house of prayer and worship.

**Congregation:** We thank Thee, O Lord, for the ____ years of blessing in this place; for the pastors, evangelists and missionaries who here have ministered Thy Word; for all the sacred memories attached to this place; for the salvation of souls and the sanctification of believers; for the fellowship of the saints; and for Thy holy presence which has attended us in this place of worship. For all these and Thy many blessings we do truly give Thee thanks.

**Pastor:** Having been challenged by the opportunities and the great responsibilities that our city presents, and recognizing the need of widening our horizon in effective service for Christ and the salvation of men, we dedicate ourselves and our possessions to the cause of Christ in this community. We shall go forward in the name of Christ, and in faith, asking and expecting great things from God.

**Closing Prayer**
**Hymn:** "Blest Be the Tie That Binds"

# 13 • Visitation

THE MINISTRY OF PASTORAL VISITATION has never been more complex, nor has it ever been more needed. The complexity is seen in several ways. First, the people of the church are very busy. It is a challenge just to find them in their homes and sufficiently rested so that they will benefit from a visit. This problem is compounded by the pastor's own schedule which will often exceed sixty hours per week. Also, people today are more cautious than in past generations. There may actually be questions about one's reason for showing pastoral concern. Finally, we must deal with a suspicious society. One is always under the threat of accusations and lawsuits, either from some dubious bystander or from the very person one seeks to help.

Ironically, the same things that bring a challenge to visitation ministry hold the reasons for its need. Individuals must know that there is a church and a minister who are offering and demonstrating the altruistic love of Christ.

The pastor who maintains a successful visitation ministry will reap rich dividends. He will have a more loyal following. His sermons will apply more practically. His church will grow numerically. And as he ministers to the needs of others, he will find himself ministered to and uplifted.

The efficiency of the visitation ministry may be enhanced by scheduling appointments. Most people appreciate the forewarning so they can have the house—

and themselves—presentable for the pastor, and it will avoid the frustration of finding no one at home.

Look for families whom you need to contact over the next week or two. Plan a convenient route, telephone the people and go out. It may help to make some calls earlier in the day. This may work particularly well with the elderly and those who are hospitalized. Then plan a certain number of evenings per month that will be used for visiting other families.

When making a visit, be sure to convey your interest in those people and their life situation. Focus on the needs, questions and dreams which are a part of their lives. But you must quickly turn the discussion to spiritual considerations. "How did you react to Sunday morning's sermon on prayer? Are you making any progress in your witness to the neighbor with the cats? What, at this point in your lives, is your greatest spiritual concern?" Avoid conversation which could lead them to think you are only interested in what they could do for the church.

As the conversation uncovers spiritual need, the minister will ask the Holy Spirit to bring to his mind a Scripture that addresses such a need. He will then read that passage aloud. Then he will pray for the family, naming each member, putting them in touch with the God who answers prayer.

And, with as few further words as possible, the minister will be on his way, leaving the family to reflect on what they heard. That is the kind of personal ministry that builds congregations.

Much of the incredulous attitude which is shown by some people will evaporate when the pastor is professional in both his appearance and his actions. Our culture has become very relaxed in the area of dress. There are times to be casual. However, when conducting your pastoral duties, proper dress is usually a good idea. That does not mean we should wear tuxedos each day. It simply means that a necktie is not a heavy burden. Although some will not care how their pastor is dressed, no one will be offended when he wears conventional dress. Just as doctors, attorneys and bankers add dignity to their position by their dress, so the minister's appearance compliments his office.

When getting together with people, whether in a home, the pastor's study or a restaurant, seek to blend caring with dignity. The warmth and interest that the shepherd feels for the sheep should be clear, though you are not their "buddy." Come with a Scripture passage that you are ready to share and with a heart that is prepared to listen. Be inclined to offer prayer with and for those you are in contact with. If the conversation reveals a larger problem, do not leap into a counseling session right there. Instead suggest that another time be set, within two or three days if possible. This will allow you to be more fully prepared.

The pastor should always be respectful of the other person's time. Do not let a visit drag on. Be careful to arrive on time. Allow several minutes for casual conversation, especially if this is the first time you have met with the family. You may wish to ask them if they have any questions or suggestions regarding the church. Then, after reading Scripture and praying, politely excuse yourself. One exception to this may be with the elderly or infirm, where some extra minutes can be very much appreciated.

Some visitation takes on an added priority. It can often be beneficial to see someone who has recently begun to attend church services. If a person has been placed in a hospital, or has just discovered that he or she has a serious physical problem, then he or she needs to hear from one of his or her Savior's representatives. Also when someone in the fellowship has experienced a loss such as a death or a divorce, he or she may appreciate a listening ear both on the anniversary of that occurrence and during holidays. Where he or she has lost a spouse, one could call on his or her anniversary or birthday. Even in times of difficulty, try to convey a real hope, while not ignoring the pain and distress the person is feeling.

The minister's procedure will be determined in part by the patient's physical condition. Sometimes he may simply quote a verse of Scripture and offer a brief prayer as he tenderly holds the hand of the person before him. In other cases, he will be at liberty to spend more time in the Word and to pray at greater length.

Ministry to one who is ill can also result in ministry to concerned family members, some of whom may be unsaved. Few acts will leave a more lasting or favorable impression on people than a pastor's concern and ministry in time of illness.

There are some cautions which should be taken in this work. As a general rule, try to avoid situations where you are isolated with just one other individual, particularly if the person has recently become single and is of the opposite sex. Try to have another person present, or at least be visible to others. If you do a lot of counseling it can be a good idea to record those sessions. If this is done, always get permission from the party to make the recording, and always keep it in close confidence.

That being said, we should also be careful about being too careful. Although it is prudent to be wary of the potential hazards of some situations, we must not allow our fears to keep us from ministering to the very people who need us the most.

The North American culture has shifted from front porches to fenced-in back patios. The sense of neighborhood has evaporated, leaving a nation filled with lonely hearts. Few acts can leave a more personal impression than when the pastor comes and demonstrates Christ's love.

**Some suggested Scriptures for specific needs:**

*For the sick:* Romans 8:18-28; James 1:2-4; Psalm 103:1-5; Matthew 8:14-17

*For the lonely:* John 14:14-18; Psalm 23:1-6

*For the distressed:* Matthew 11:28-30; Isaiah 43:1-3; Psalm 107:28-31

*For the guilty:* John 8:1-11; Psalm 51:11-13; Hebrews 4:14-16

*For the frightened:* Genesis 15:1; Isaiah 41:10; 2 Corinthians 1:3-7

# *Appendix*

## *Themes of the Christian Year*

| | |
|---|---|
| 1st Sunday of Advent | The Hope of His Coming |
| 2nd Sunday of Advent | The Prophecy of His Coming |
| 3rd Sunday of Advent | The Preparation of His Coming |
| 4th Sunday of Advent | The Annunciation of His Coming |
| Christmas Eve | The Birth of Christ |
| Christmas 1 | The Angelic Proclamation |
| Christmas 2 (Epiphany) | The Magi |
| Christmas 3 | The Baptism of Christ |
| Christmas 4 | The Disciples |
| Christmas 5 | The Signs of His Messiahship |
| Christmas 6 | The Sermon on the Mount |
| Christmas 7 | Christ and Sinners |
| Christmas 8 | Christ the Healer |
| Christmas 9 | Christ the Teacher (His Parables) |
| Ash Wednesday | Humility and Self-examination |

| | |
|---|---|
| 1st Sunday of Lent | The Transfiguration |
| 2nd Sunday of Lent | The Promise of the Holy Spirit |
| 3rd Sunday of Lent | The Prayers of Christ |
| 4th Sunday of Lent | Opposition to the Kingdom of God |
| 5th Sunday of Lent (Passion Sunday) | The Temptations of Christ |
| 6th Sunday of Lent (Palm Sunday) | The Way to the Cross |
| Maundy Thursday | The Last Passover |
| Good Friday | The Death of Christ |
| Resurrection (Easter) Day | The Resurrection of Christ |
| Easter 1 | The Proof of Resurrection |
| Easter 2 | The Appearances of Christ |
| Easter 3 | Doubt and Denial |
| Easter 4 | The Good Shepherd |
| Easter 5 | The Great Commission |
| Ascension Day | The Ascension of Christ |
| Ascension Sunday | The Intercession of Christ |
| Pentecost (Whitsuntide) | The Baptism of the Spirit |
| Pentecost 1 (Trinity Sunday) | The Trinity The Attributes of God |
| Pentecost 2 | The People of God Election |

| | |
|---|---|
| Pentecost 3 | Baptism<br>Atonement |
| Pentecost 4 | Freedom from the Law<br>Salvation |
| Pentecost 5 | The New Law<br>Assurance |
| Pentecost 6 | The Man in Christ<br>Justification |
| Pentecost 7 | The Fullness of the Spirit<br>Regeneration |
| Pentecost 8 | The Fruit of the Spirit<br>Adoption |
| Pentecost 9 | The Whole Armor of God<br>Redemption |
| Pentecost 10 | The Gifts of the Spirit<br>Sanctification |
| Pentecost 11 | The Serving Community<br>Grace |
| Pentecost 12 | The Witnessing Community<br>Faith |
| Pentecost 13 | The Suffering Community<br>Perseverance |
| Pentecost 14 | Love Your Neighbor<br>Providence |
| Pentecost 15 | The Family<br>The Church |
| Pentecost 16 | Authority<br>The Sacraments |

| | |
|---|---|
| Pentecost 17 | Proof of Faith<br>Prayer |
| Pentecost 18 | Tithes and Offerings<br>Mortality |
| Pentecost 19 | Life of Faith<br>The Last Days |
| Pentecost 20 | Millennial Reign<br>The Resurrection of the Dead |
| Pentecost 21 | Citizens of Heaven<br>The Final Judgment |
| Pentecost 22 | Creation |
| Pentecost 23 | The Fall |
| Pentecost 24 | Types of Salvation: Noah and the Flood, Joseph |
| Pentecost 25 | God's Chosen People Abraham and Isaac, Moses |
| Pentecost 26 | Salvation History: Ezra and Nehemiah, Joshua |

In this thematic outline, two themes are given for the Sundays of Pentecost, so that by alternating years, the themes relative to the church and the Christian life can be presented.